D1606437

Where Souls Meet

Caring for
the seriously ill

Dillon Woods

Editorial, sales and distribution, rights and permissions inquiries should be addressed to Windermere Publications, P.O. Box 25109, Los Angeles, California 90025 Tel. 310/358-6043

Windermere Publication books may be purchased in bulk at special discounts for sales promotions, fund-raising, or educational purposes. Special editions can be created to specifications. For details, contact Special Sales Department, Windermere Publications, P.O. Box 25109, Los Angeles, CA 90025 310/358-6043

Dillon Woods
C/O Windermere Publications
P.O. Box 25109; Los Angeles, CA 90025
Phone: 310/358-6043
For email, go to the website at www.livingwithquality.com

Manufactured in the United States of America
ISBN 0-9705981-1-4

Edited by Paul Haber
Graphic Design by Amy Hayes & Jessica L. Ikenberry

Edition two
Printed August 2002

This book is dedicated to those who helped me learn about life and death by allowing me to share a part of their journey. A percentage of the proceeds from this book will go to various charitable organizations and hospices.

Written on a tomb stone:

Dear friend,
Know that as you pass by, so once was I.
As I am now, so you will be.
Prepare yourself to follow me.

CONTENTS

UNTIL THE DAY I DIE...

I have the need to be treated with the knowledge and respect that this is my life. Until the day I die, I am still an individual and it's right for me to be part of the decisions that concern my care.

Try to let the terminally ill person do things their way. Always ask for their preference when a decision needs to be made. Do not force your will on them. Trust that they will let you know how they want to deal with a situation. If they are not being clear, feel free to ask questions and encourage a discussion. Do not judge any decisions a patient has made that you disagree with.

I need to keep a feeling of hope alive in my heart, no matter the circumstances.

Talk about how great something in the future will be. Remind your loved one of what they have to look forward to. Create moments for them to look forward to. Sit with them, walk, and hold their hand while they face the toughest battle of their life.

I need to feel you are the friend you have always been. I need your presence in my life frequently.

Don't avoid a dying friend. At least call and talk a little. Often people may not know what to say, so they stay away completely. Those who are ill may not always have the energy to have long conversations, so a short conversation will probably be welcome, anyway. It's always nice to hear a friendly voice and be reminded that someone loves you and is thinking of you. Even if you can't be with them often, the flowers, cards and cookies you bring stay with them when you leave.

Some things you might do: call for a shopping list, ask if you can visit for lunch, ask if they feel like talking that day (don't be afraid to ask if they feel like talking about what they're going through).

Help the family and children; this is very hard for them too. A seriously ill person needs help from the family in accepting their death and they also need help for the family in accepting their death. At holiday time, join in the celebration by helping to decorate their room. Bring a book of your favorite quotes, or music, or a homemade tape of inspirational readings. Your loved one needs you. They are probably very lonely and afraid.

I need to be touched, but please ask permission before you touch too long.

Simply touching a hand or giving a hug can help give support at this time when they feel so alone. However, there are moments when emotional and physical space is necessary. Don't be hurt if they want to be alone.

I have the need to express my feelings freely.

Support your loved one regardless of whether they laugh or cry. Both laughter and tears of sadness are especially important at this time. Any help you can be to bringing more of this into the life of an ill person is always a welcomed breath of fresh air.

I need a break from this world of healthcare.

Their whole life is consumed with doctors, disease and medications. Any extra time you can spare to take a sick friend out for a walk, a cup of coffee, lunch, or a movie is always appreciated. Give the patient a vacation from their world as much as you can.

I sometimes need to simply sit in silence.

An ill person may not always feel the need to talk. Often there are times when it's nice to just have someone in the room. Sometimes no words are necessary to express what is being felt. Welcome silence.

I have the need for honesty from you and all those in my life.

Seriously ill people do not need deception. When they ask a question, they deserve a truthful answer regardless of the issue.

I may need to discuss my religious views.

Allow this to be done with anyone they choose.

I get to choose whom I want and need around me.

Don't feel hurt or take it personally if you are not asked for, or if your offer for lunch is turned down. This probably means that there is a feeling of closure and fulfillment with you. They may need to use the remainder of their energy and time to have closure with others in their life also.

INTRODUCTION

I was barely out of my teenage years when the desire to become a Franciscan Monk hit me. As I pursued my Masters of Divinity degree I became a member of a monastery, and followed their rule of life intensely while I continued my studies. Even though I was a "monk-in-training," people who were ill often approached me for prayer. During this time I learned of the many people who flock to church and religion in times of despair, desperation, fear and suffering. It took me only a short time to realize that everyone wants to go to "heaven", but no one wants to die!

While living in the monastery my first superior, Father Chris Dobson, T.O.R. said I had become overly spiritual and felt that I needed more balance in my life. His exact words were, "You've become so heavenly minded that you are no earthly good." To give me more practical life experience, he asked me to work as a chaplain in a local hospital. He believed this kind of work was what I needed to bring me back to the reality of this world. Although hesitant at first (did I really want to be around sick people?), I enjoyed the job. So, at 22-years of age I was the chaplain's assistant at Mercy Hospital. I felt I was able to make a positive difference in the lives of those I met and those with whom I worked.

While at this hospital, I met and worked with Sister Dorothy Kline, R.S.M. It was she, more than anyone, who taught me the art of working with those who were ill. She was a tiny person, but she had the biggest heart, and eyes that danced with excitement, inspiration and positive energy. Her one passion was what she called "clown ministry." To this day she dedicates her life to making people (especially kids) smile. As the head chaplin, she helped to shape my early thinking and experience with death, suffering and illness. Through Sister Dorothy I learned to listen to others from my heart. This was a skill I had, up to that point, given little thought to. *"Listening is a skill to be learned, practiced and mastered,"* she said. *"The easiest rule to remember is the most important. Listen the way you want to be listened to."* No one listened like Sister Dorothy.

iv

After leaving the monastery, I was forced to learn about serious illness in a completely new way. Suddenly illness and I had a different, more personal, relationship, as I helped both my parents while they were in their battle with cancer. They died within a few months of each other. I thought I had been prepared for this experience, with all I had learned in the monastery and in the hospital with Sister Dorothy. I had been a spiritual leader; I had helped countless numbers of families deal with exactly this issue; I was a professional. No problem, I thought. I was wrong. I was surprised to find the experience of losing my parents wrenching and deeply upsetting in ways I hadn't anticipated. However, I knew I was more fortunate than most because I had at least a few things on which I could rely; for instance, my education on this subject and my years of experience in being of service to others.

Luckily, I'm a note taker. I keep notes and journals for virtually every occasion. In caring for my parents I would often refer to some of the notes I had taken while in the monastery. The messages spoken so clearly by my Franciscan mentors and Sister Dorothy reminded me to see that death is as natural a process in life as birth. Ironically, I found myself searching for advice that I had once so easily given mournful family members. During this difficult time I was also able to bond more deeply to my siblings and I ultimately experienced a sort of transformation in the outlook of my own life.

In retrospect, one of the things that helped my transformation happen was the hospice workers I met during my parent's battle with cancer. They were trained to help in situations like that of my family, so it was arranged that they would help us care for my parents. Hospice came to my parent's home with a quiet presence, yet they quickly gained our respect and trust. Whether it's hospice volunteers or friends and family, it is necessary to have someone available so you can get away for a day or even just a few hours. The last few months of someone's life are very difficult for everyone in the situation – even paid nurses. I was so impressed by my experience with hospice, that when my grief was mostly healed, I sought to give back and I became a hospice volunteer in Los Angeles.

Because of my background in psychology and spirituality, I was asked by the Hospice Program at a hospital in Los Angeles, California to teach a class to volunteers called *Communicating with the Seriously Ill.* I found that through teaching others I became more aware of the abundance of knowledge I had on this subject. I was able to not only give those in the class what they needed, but was also able to relearn it myself.

As the class progressed these notes grew into a small booklet and this small booklet continued to expand. I eventually began providing copies to friends and hospice workers I knew who were in the process of being with a seriously ill person. The response was tremendous and encouraging. The book you hold now was sparked by the suggestions of those readers.

Where Souls Meet was written in an effort to provide guidance, understanding, and comfort to anyone struggling through this difficult, yet universal experience.

On one level, this publication is a guide to the etiquette of being with someone who is seriously ill. It's also a reflective look at end-of-life issues. I offer many suggestions - and hopefully a few insights - taken directly from my own experiences. Each idea you see in these pages may not translate directly into every situation. But by considering the ideas in this book, may you be guided to your own insights for your own situation.

CHAPTER 1

STAGES

Being with the seriously ill can bring many positive things into our lives. It can, however, also bring on a feeling of oppressive despair that colors life in a tone of melancholy. Suddenly everything looks different. Priorities change. You reevaluate everything. You see how short life is. You want to sleep all the time or you get no sleep at all. You lose 15 pounds or you gain 15 pounds. Make no mistake about it – holding the hand of someone as they die is a very, very difficult thing to do. The process wears many people down everyday.

It is not surprising that the "deathwatch" often turns into an earnest, prayerful vigil for a swift end. The journey also brings a variety of stages and emotions for the dying person. Dr. Elizabeth Kubler-Ross author of *On Death and Dying*, has carefully explained many of these stages. The stages of dying she focused on were denial, anger, bargaining, depression, and acceptance.

According to many of the hospice professionals I interviewed as part of my research for this book, it is generally believed that these stages do not always occur in every case. If they do all occur, they do not seem to appear in any sequential or predictable pattern. Some patients may be stuck on one stage for 90 percent of their time. More often, however, patients seem to go back and forth between a few of the stages.

As a loved one or caretaker, it's important that you do not judge a stage as good or bad. It is what it is: a stage, a moment. Focus on how you can support the person at whatever stage they find themselves and avoid tampering with that stage or their defense mechanisms. In one stage, someone may feel a tremendous amount of anger towards the situation. In another stage, they may turn to religion and hope to strike a deal with God.

I have observed that a significant number of seriously ill patients go through yet another stage in which they feel strengthened when they nurture their inner spirit. I call this stage "connecting." They connect in a variety of subtle activities: taking time to notice the beauty of nature, taking time for meditation, consciously appreciating the kindness of people in their lives, relating to people in a more genuine way, and speaking to loved ones and to God with deeper sincerity.

STAGES OF THE CARETAKER

Many people in our modern day society are uncomfortable with end of life issues. In working on your own acceptance of these issues, your helping someone through the process and your being-helped by the process will begin to intersect. If you have someone in your life that is very ill now, you may think you are here to help them at this very difficult point in their life. The truth is, this experience will do more for you (in helping you grow spiritually and emotionally), than you could ever do for anyone who is very ill. I strongly believe the best way to work on spiritual growth is to help and be with someone who is seriously ill. Be there with your heart and you will never be the same. Here are some stages you might go through as a caretaker.

Fear

Often when someone begins helping a seriously ill person, they begin with a sense of insecurity. *"Will I know what to say or do? Do I have the energy or time this will demand?"*

The Honeymoon

After moving beyond fear and getting a few weeks under your belt, a feeling of confidence may eventually fill your days. It feels good to do things for others. There is often a feeling of honest connection and closeness with the ill person. This often brings a strong feeling of self-esteem as you realize how good it is to help someone in such a situation.

The Roller Coaster

Some days you'll get home and collapse from exhaustion, or perhaps the patient's depression rubs off on you. By now, your bonding with the patient has solidified, and you may be sharing in their headaches, stress, and tension. This is when it's most important to focus on self-care (chapter four discusses this in greater detail).

Letting Go

There comes a time when the caregiver needs to let go. After taking such an intense journey with another human being, it is understandable that this is a very difficult thing to do. Maintaining a high level of care for the patient, while at the same time being mindful of your own self-care is very important. You may want to take time to process your feelings by writing them down in a journal, talking with family and friends or joining a support group for caretakers (a local hospice or hospital may have a support group). More than ever, you need support at this time.

Relief & Guilt

If the ill person you are helping does eventually die, it is common to have conflicting feelings. *"I'm so relieved this is over."* is often followed by *"What am I saying?!"*… Which is then followed by, *"I wish she was still here."* Or *"I really miss him."* Everyone's timetable for processing feelings of grief and loss is different. Don't be too hard on yourself and try not to set a limit as to the amount of time it will take to heal. Healing is different for each person. There is no "normal" number of days or weeks or years. When it's time you'll know – and you'll let go.

CHAPTER 2

PAUL

When I arrived, Paul was in and out of a deep sleep. Upon taking my first steps into his sterile room I met a caretaker named George, he had been Paul's handyman/gardener for many years. It was clear from the moment I met him, George was not just an employee, but also a devoted family friend.

Paul's children had placed him in a nursing home because they could not give him the dedicated care he needed, and they found his serious illness and impending death difficult to watch.

I, like George, was asked to visit Paul in this nursing home in which he had been placed only a week prior. It seemed that Paul had a good arrangement. The family had hired 24-hour caretakers in addition to the 24-hour nurses that were on staff at the nursing home. His children wanted to be sure that dad "always knew someone was there for him" – as he had always been there for so many.

George would quietly sit in the room and read or watch TV. The family felt that Paul would appreciate a familiar face when he woke up. However, as George sat in his chair at the opposite end of the room, it was obvious that he was not thrilled about spending his days in a nursing home with a dying friend. He was literally in Paul's room, but physically as far away from Paul as possible.

When George left, I took his place in the chair. I thought perhaps he was sitting this far away from Paul at his request. Once Paul finally woke up I introduced myself and asked if he wouldn't mind if I moved the chair right next to his bed. He said that would be OK, so I moved the chair closer and then placed my right hand on the bed within Paul's reach, just in case he wanted to touch. We talked a little and before I knew it he had brought his hand on top of mine and just gave it a light squeeze. The more time I spent with him, the more I came to see how starved for affection he really was.

When Paul was awake, he would often reach over and touch my hand. We would talk about whatever he had the energy for or interest in. Once in a while I would ask a question, *"Are you in any pain?" "Are you thirsty?" "Is there anyone you'd like to see or talk to today?"*

We had some really great conversations in those last days. We talked about his favorite hobby (fly fishing), what it was like being a father, what his kids were like, his grandkids, what he did for work, and so on. He was still working on the inventory of his life and would sometimes talk on and on until he put himself to sleep. I just listened, nodded my head and asked an occasional question.

I sincerely enjoyed spending time with Paul. Since the nursing home where he stayed was only minutes from my apartment, I was able to spend some time with him every day. I began to feel that he was approaching his final days, because his breathing pattern had drastically changed. His body was just worn out. Sometimes when he was awake, I sensed his loneliness, apprehension, and at times, his fear.

One day I walked in and he was sitting up in bed looking pained, watching TV.

"Hello," he said.

"Hey, Paul." We shook hands.

"Are you in any pain today?" He shook his head,

"No."

We talked a little more and he eventually dozed off to sleep. Again, I moved the chair by Paul's bed and put my hand by his. I sat there reading and thinking. Two hours later, Paul woke up for a few minutes and we had a moment I will never forget.

He leaned up in bed and looked at me with his gaunt face and drawn, yet vibrant, eyes. He grabbed my hand and held it tight. I could tell from his eyes that he was searching for either the words or the energy to speak. Once our eyes connected, we were suspended in a moment that was profoundly silent. Finally, looking at me with the deepest sincerity in his eyes, he said: *"I know what you're doing...and I want you to know...I really appreciate it."*

I could say nothing for about 10 seconds (which seemed like an eternity) as his words and eyes made their impression on me. I was stunned by his genuineness and humility. Paul died the next day - one hour before my next scheduled time to be with him. The nursing staff said he simply stopped breathing in his sleep. He was 96 years old.

Change is the breath of God. It is the pulsing force of intense creativity constantly expressing itself.

CHAPTER 3

DEALING WITH LOSS

Change is a constant theme in life, isn't it? With every changing event there is the excitement of possibility unknown and the loss of something remembered. Our loss starts early in life. We lose our teeth, maybe our teenage innocence, and maybe even a parent or a grandparent along the way. We move away from home and lose our familiar nest. Loss is a constant theme and all these losses provide us with a great opportunity. They prepare us for the biggest and final loss.

If we acknowledge, work through and accept our small losses now, we will be more prepared to deal with the biggest and final losses of our life when that time comes. By embracing change and loss as a gift of life, I believe we ensure a greater chance of weathering the storm of serious illness with a sense of peace and serenity.

Some additional issues that arise at the end of life might be issues of control, brutal honesty, self-pity, letting go, sadness, inner-peace, renewed faith, and fear. If you are afraid of the dying process or you are insecure about issues that are central to death, you may be less effective as a helper. I don't say this to discourage you. But the reality is, the more attentive you are to your own self-growth and inner life, the more helpful you will be on this difficult journey that requires much inner strength.

Some people come to work with the seriously ill and feel afraid, uneasy or nervous. The only thing you really need to be effective is love in your heart and openness to all the lessons that will come to you. Once you have this love and openness within yourself, you are prepared to participate with someone in their difficult and possibly their final journey. There's no need to be nervous. Simply listen to them. By listening intently and following the cues that you are given by them, you will find the ways in which you can be most helpful.

For example, if someone is talking to you and you notice that a theme keeps reoccurring, that is something I would ask them more about. Let them talk it all out. The bottom line is, by listening from your heart and following your inner compass you will find your way in a place you've never been before. Trust the goodness that is inside you, for it is this goodness that is drawing you to be helpful in the first place. (I'll be talking more about this in Chapter 7, Listening 101.)

There is a large amount of inner strength, generosity and maturity needed to be with someone who is seriously ill. Again, the importance of taking care of yourself is paramount. The more you have your center and connection to your inner self, the more helpful you will be to someone else.

If you are steadily giving to someone who is seriously ill, you must take time to replenish your own energy. It is wearisome work. Find time – consistently – for yourself. Take time to relax and enjoy life. Do something you love to do now and then. It's not wrong to have some fun even though your loved one is very ill. (I know from my own life, this is easier said than done.) So often, people let guilt or depression hold them back from living their lives. As best you can, don't let that happen! It's okay to enjoy life! Nurture yourself. Care for yourself. Embrace life and be appreciative of all the things you enjoy, all the things you are able to do, and all the things you have. Someday, the time will come to let go of these things. But, for now, enjoy them! Give yourself time to experience some of the beauty and pleasures of life. Don't forget to enjoy the little things!

Also keep in mind, the more you take care of yourself, the more you will have to give to the person you are caring for. You do them no good when you're emotionally and physically depleted. Make a contract with yourself to care for and nurture yourself, as well as your loved one. The truth is, if you truly want them to be well taken care of; you can do it best by taking care of yourself first!

When helping the seriously ill,
the questions are basic:

What would you like?
When would you like it?
Where would you like it?
Who would you like it from?

CHAPTER 4

REACHING A COMFORT LEVEL

Before being comfortable in the presence of someone who is seriously ill, coming to terms with your own limits and your own mortality are concepts that will help make you a more effective and empathetic caretaker. This means being aware and accepting of your own eventual decline and death – unavoidable subjects when caring for someone who is ill.

One method I've used to gain comfort and self-knowledge in this area is by meditating on it. But there are many ways to reflect and gain a healthy perspective on death. For you, it may mean just thinking about it, not shying away from the thoughts when they enter your consciousness. Reading books, having conversations with others, and holding the hand of someone who is seriously ill are all great ways to grow in this area. The topic of death is never easy for anyone, but the dying process seems to be easiest for those who, during their life, give the issue some reflection and preparation. There is a well-known tombstone inscription that reads:

Dear Friend,
Know that as you pass by, so once was I.
As I am now, so you will be.
Prepare yourself to follow me.

By living lives that are at the service of someone who is seriously ill, we are not only helping another person. But, we are doing something to help our own future have a sense of depth and clarity. Two additional things that help make this experience less difficult are 1) a lifestyle of humility and 2) the practice of "consciously letting go." We learn lessons of humility by learning to let go. Again, letting go of small things in life will help prepare us for the final, big letting go.

Generally speaking, people who have lived an entire life focused on power and control have a very difficult time at the end of their life. No one can control everyone or everything. Accepting that as fact and focusing on service to others, will allow us to learn those lessons of humility, which can often defuse the need to control.

Regularly being mindful of our eventual death will also help us experience life more fully because it gives us the constant awareness that it can end at any moment. Remember that it doesn't matter how long we live – but in what we do with the time that we have. Some folks live a long life, but never fully live, so what's the point? When reflecting on death, you learn to die, but more importantly, you learn to live.

Every once in a while, when I have an important decision to make, I do something to help me through the decision-making process. I go to a local cemetery and walk very slowly around the grounds reading tombstones and thinking about the decision to be made. The unconscious message in doing this says, this is where I'm going to end up. So, in light of this, how important is this decision really? What is my gut telling me to do? With that end in mind, answers to troubling questions have a way of coming perfectly clear to me.

When strolling in a garden of tombstones, you gain clarity of vision. When you hold the hand of someone who might be dying, clarity of mind comes to you. You see everything differently.

Historically, some monks have meditated on death by putting a human skull on their desk as a constant, daily reminder that death is part of life, and life is very short. (For the record, in my years as a

Franciscan, I never kept a skull on my desk. But I do walk in cemeteries when I have a big decision to make. Most people think that's unusual enough.)

COMFORT THROUGH PLANNING

A smart businessperson starts a business by first assessing the desired outcome. What is the objective of the pursuit? Once the goal is assessed, it's time to then sit down and design a business plan, a strategy to get there. While business plans may consist of a variety of different categories depending on the focus of the work, there are always similarities. Most business plans consist of the following:

- Company Description
- Management Plan
- Services
- Operating Plan

Finding comfort though a plan uses the same basic concept. It's about deliberately choosing a lifestyle that is consistent with all that you learn when you are with the seriously ill. Although the process may differ with each caretaker as well as with each ill person, there will be topics that are consistent in the majority of cases:

- Mission Statement
- Skills I Bring to the Table
- Acknowledging My Weaknesses
- Taking Care of Myself

It's important to remember that it doesn't matter so much how you study the topic of death and dying – but that you do study it, think about it, mull it over somehow. There are many ways to reflect and prepare for our eventual end or the eventual end of those we love. One of the by-products of preparing for the future in this way, is that it makes your present moments more delicious... more invigorating. *Carpe Diem* – Seize the Day – takes on a depth of new energy and meaning.

Let's explore the Comfort Plan. You may find it helpful to write down the ideas discussed in this section. Creating your own Comfort Plan will help the ideas behind this theory sink in and can then provide clarity. You may also find it helpful to have something to refer to when times get really difficult. Sometimes we don't think so clearly when we are overwhelmed and stressed. Reading and re-reading your personal Comfort Plan will remind you of your end goal, which can alleviate the sensations of confusion, anger, exhaustion or hurt feelings that may arise when working with a seriously ill loved one.

The ideas mentioned in the next few paragraphs are offered simply as guidelines – where to begin. Although the main subject headings should be addressed, the way in which they are addressed is at your own discretion. Remember, this is your Comfort Plan. What works best for you is the only important thing.

i. Mission Statement

I am dedicated to the comfort and health of all beings, including my own being. I understand the importance of helping those in need, but it can't be done at the expense of my health and well-being.

ii. Skills I Bring to the Table

I have the following skills that will help others and some that will help me remain calm and may relieve tension when I am feeling overwhelmed. The skills you list here may include things like using humor, prayer, an ability to remain clear-headed under stress, etc.

iii. Acknowledging My Weaknesses

I know that there are many skills I need to work on to help me through this difficult time. These skills are somewhere deep within me, and if I acknowledge them I can begin to bring strength to them. These skills might include things like: a fear of hospitals, fear of death, a lack of faith, impatience, the ability to communicate with someone who isn't very talkative, etc.

iv. Taking Care of Myself

I will begin to help myself when I am overwhelmed and tense by first taking a few deep, cleansing breaths and then by doing one of the following activities: (this list of activities should include things that you consider fun, refreshing, relaxing or pampering, like going to the gym, getting a massage, spending time alone or with good friends who are not involved with the ill person, etc.) THIS IS VERY IMPORTANT!

When you're feeling stressed or overwhelmed refer to this list. It will comfort you, and help ground you.

"To die is poignantly bitter.
But, the idea of having to die
without having ever lived is unbearable."

— Erich Fromm

CHAPTER 5

DENIAL

I was caring for a cancer patient named John who was confined to a wheelchair. John insisted that he walk his dog, Sofie, a large German Shepherd. *"I can do it myself,"* he would exclaim. So, I agreed that he could "walk" Sofie while I followed discretely behind. In case there was a problem. It was a beautiful summer day and the sky was clear and blue. Sofie was walking along, gently pulling the wheelchair behind her. *"I guess this wasn't such a bad idea after all,"* I thought.

Suddenly, a fluffy white cat ran in front of Sofie and, you can imagine what happened! The dog took off! To make matters worse, John had tied the leash to his wheelchair, so now both he and Sofie were chasing that cat down the street. Luckily I was not far behind and caught up with them before anything bad happened. What's the moral to this story?

MORAL #1: Patients need to feel like they are living as normal a life as possible. They will push to do things as they have always done them. Let them do this, but be close at hand to help, should help be needed. As they slowly lose their ability to function, help will be needed at some point.

MORAL #2: Be patient. Let them do as much for themselves as they can. Yes, it's faster if you rush in there and do it for them. But, it makes us feel better if we can do it for ourselves.

MORAL #3: Never tie a dog leash to a wheelchair.

DEALING WITH DENIAL

We can take only as much as we can take. Who is to judge where that limit is for you or for me? Some people confuse denial with lying. But, denial is nothing like a lie. They are not the same thing at all. Lying is deliberate and conscious, but denial is a subconscious coping mechanism.

Psychologically, there are things we all create to help us deal with whatever crisis or stress comes our way. We all have our ways of coping with reality. Denial is meant to be a cushion from the shock of a difficult experience. If denial were a person in your life, it would be both a close friend, while at the same time a hated enemy. It is the perfect example of a paradox because it insulates while it obstructs at the same time.

In most cases, denial is a byproduct of intense fear. In these situations, it may be easy for denial to cross over into psychosis, as people need to live in denial because the shock is too much for them to bear. Denial helps them break down the intense shock a little at a time. It's easier for most of us to accept things in small doses. If someone needs to be in denial, that's fine. Denial is that inner protection that comes from a place deep within the psyche. To disrupt that protection process would not only be disrespectful to the individual, but probably harmful as well.

When the patient is living in denial, it can make it harder on the family members and loved ones. When there is not any honest connection or conversation about the situation as it really is, it can become an even more difficult experience for everyone. Real feelings are not free to express themselves. It can be a very frustrating experience for everyone involved.

Further, denial makes it very difficult for the seriously ill person to participate in the decisions that must be made in the last days. Those decisions are the ones that might help bring about closure and allow for a more peaceful end, rather than an end filled with stress.

Denial can also make it difficult for you, the caretaker, to help prepare someone for what lies ahead. To live in denial and not, for example, put all our affairs in order, is a bad idea. It takes tact and strategy to help a person in denial come to accept the various stages of their progressive disease. They may never want to accept that they will eventually need a walker, a wheelchair, and then be bed-ridden. But with thoughtfulness on our part, and respect for the denial, we can sometimes help someone to see the positive aspects of whatever their present situation is.

I once knew someone who was in the early stages of cancer, and he was in complete denial. He hated the word "wheelchair." Whenever it would come up in a conversation or when he saw one on the television or the street, he made his feelings very clear. He would never go in a wheelchair. As time went by, however, his walking got worse and he needed more than a walker or cane to get around. His friends would always ask me, *"What can we do?"*

I started to suggest that if the idea of a wheelchair ever came up in a conversation, they might subtly mention positive aspects of using one. It took several months, but the gentle campaign actually worked. Thereafter, whenever it came up, his friends would say something positive about using a wheelchair. *"Think of how easy it would be to travel in airports!" "You'd be able to get out more." "A wheelchair will get us around museums more quickly!"* All these points began to look attractive, and when it came time for the transition, it was made smoothly and on an upbeat note. In a situation like this, I would also caution about being overly optimistic in your language; from an ill person's perspective, sometimes the well-meaning optimism of perfectly healthy people around them can be a negative experience.

For some people in denial, they especially don't want to be treated as if they're dying – they want to be treated as if they're sick and soon everything will be fine. This can be very hard for family members and friends to play along with, because you can see what the ill person refuses to acknowledge. But it's important to support a patient's denial if that's how the patient needs to handle it.

CHAPTER 6

BEING NON-JUDGMENTAL

To communicate most effectively with someone who is seriously ill, it's important to be present with them as they are, not as we wish they were. If we go into their world with our own fears, our own way of how we think things should be done—in other words, our own judgments—it can impede us from being a truly effective helper. Judgment is an emotional roadblock to compassionate care. The hardest thing about this issue is that we don't usually recognize ourselves as being judgmental.

In the words of one friend: *"I hate judgmental people."* He didn't realize he was being humorous, since his statement was in itself a judgment. Even when we come from a position of love, judgments can creep in, and can hold us back from being a truly helpful caretaker.

If we go into the ill person's world with our own expectations, our own fears, our own way of how we think things should be done, it may keep us from understanding what the ill person is really saying.

There are many different ways in which being judgmental impairs our ability to connect deeply with someone. Let's look at some common judgments caregivers may experience. You may even recognize yourself in some of these examples. Just be careful not to have any judgments about yourself for being judgmental!

1. Judgments can take the form of impatience when our loved one attempts simple tasks.

There may be moments when the ill person does not do something exactly right or what we consider "right" and it's tempting to correct them. This sort of judgment and criticism can be a fragile foundation on which to build a helping relationship. The ill person may, at times, seem unable to do common activities – reaching for something, turning the television on, holding the telephone. If it seems clear that the ill person wants to try to do things for themselves, take a deep breath and let them. Even if you think (or know) that they can't do something, let them try. Even if you think you can do it faster. Remember, at a time when the ill person may feel overwhelmed by a feeling of powerlessness over their life, tiny activities may offer a small measure of satisfaction, accomplishment and control.

I can remember one friend of mine telling me about a heated argument he had with his brother because their terminally ill mother wanted to go to the mall to do some window shopping. She had been very sick for several weeks. The chemo treatments had left her with no hair and little strength. She was now wearing a wig and learning to use a wheelchair.

This particular day was a good one and she was feeling a little stronger. She was tired of being in the house, so she asked her sons to take her out. My friend's brother said: *"Mom should stay home. She looks like hell and she needs to save her strength."* My friend's response was, *"Save her strength for what!? This would give her some enjoyment. Let's take her."* Fortunately, they came to an understanding and were glad they went to the mall because later that day she made several references to what a wonderful time she had when they went out. She passed away only a few weeks later.

Small excursions (like an hour at the mall) can give a seriously ill person some badly needed time out of the house. Small judgments like, *"She looks like hell"* can be the exact thing that keeps us from really connecting with and helping our loved one. Although it didn't happen with my friend and his brother, these judgments have the potential to blow up and cause breaks in family relationships. If you truly worry that an outing would do more harm than good, consult with their healthcare professional first.

2. Along the same line, another judgment may take place when seeing the physical appearance of a seriously ill person. This is especially true when seeing someone for the first time after some of the stages of incremental decline have taken place. Often times, people are shocked when they see the physical changes in a person. In some cases, it doesn't take very long to happen. Give them the freedom they need to look less than perfect. They may not have the strength or inclination to worry about how they look.

If you're with someone who wants help in looking better, another judgment trap is to tell them they don't need it. You may even think: who will see them, what difference does it make? But it may make a big difference to them. If you're asked to help, don't hesitate to jump right in. It may make them feel better to have their hair styled, be freshly shaved, or wear some jewelry or perfume.

Remember, it's about how the patient feels about him or herself. Spending time helping someone get "fixed up" can be a wonderful expression of love. It also helps create bonding moments you might never forget.

3. A big challenge for some caregivers is the first time a seriously ill person loses control of their bowels. This is a common occurrence, and in most cases, it should be expected to happen at some point. For the person that it is happening to, it is an extremely embarrassing moment. The loss of control, the loss of dignity, the unpleasant odor and asking someone to clean the mess is enough to deal with, not to mention the feeling of complete helplessness. How the caretaker reacts can make all the difference in how they feel when they have this experience.

Another friend of mine was caring for his mom in her final days, when she lost control of her bowels. She was humiliated to have the nurse find her that way. My friend (her son) rolled up his sleeves and said he'd help clean her up. At first, his mother refused. She said she couldn't have him do that. But he looked her right in the eye and said: *"Mom, you changed my shitty diapers for nearly two years. This is the least I can do for you."* His calm willingness to do the difficult work was reassuring to her, and she allowed him to help (and in doing so, the relationship came full circle).

The seriously ill person will often take their cue from you, to see how you'll react to situations that arise. If you're calm, forthright and willing to metaphorically 'roll up your sleeves' during difficult moments, that can be very reassuring to someone who is seriously ill. No one wants to feel like a burden. Your ready willingness to help without hesitation can be the very thing that will make them feel that it's OK for them to accept help.

In a situation like my friend experienced with his mom, it's possible the ill person may prefer a stranger like a nurse or another caregiver not so close to them to clean them up. The key is to help them in the way they want, and to assure them that their decisions, their preferences, will be respected.

4. Another judgment is that death is bad, or how awful it is that they're sick at all.

Many of us have heard statements similar to this: *"How horrible it is for this young 29-year-old mother to have to go through this cancer treatment."*

The statement may indeed be an accurate one, but it might not be helpful when trying to comfort a patient. Yes, the situation may be difficult, perhaps even horrible, but as a caregiver, spending time and energy judging what is good or bad, or what is right or wrong, ultimately won't help the ill person – and helping is ultimately the primary concern.

If you communicate these ideas to the seriously ill person, even in the subtlest of ways or with an unconscious pitying glance, they will pick up on it. This is their illness, and maybe even their death process, and they may have specific ideas about how they see it all unfolding.

On some level, I think once we make these judgments, we place ourselves outside the situation and are not being present in the situation with the ill person. If we are as present as we can be to the moment and the person, then we are in a position to better facilitate a comforting presence.

5. Another judgment can be wrapped in the pious cloth of religion or spirituality. Imposing religious or spiritual beliefs on someone can completely impede your ability to be an effective caretaker.

You may think you know the truth about the hereafter. You may also be certain that the seriously ill person would have an easier passing (and hereafter) if only they believed what you believed. And you may be correct. But each of us has the right to our own religious or spiritual beliefs. The seriously ill person is on a journey and a path that we must honor, even if we think we know a "better" way for them. If we truly want to help someone who is ill, we must respect their beliefs, no matter how they differ from ours.

6. Speaking in a condescending manner can hinder our ability to connect with someone who is seriously ill. Talking to the ill person as if they were a child or talking in a patronizing tone are ways in which we might block effective communication with our loved one. And it can make a seriously ill person feel even worse about themselves.

I don't think most people even know they're doing this. It can be an unconscious way of communicating. Talking to an adult as a child can be a way of emotionally distancing ourselves when we are uncomfortable with what is going on. Speak to them with respect and care as you would any other adult, and you will, in this way, keep the ground fertile for open, heart-felt communication.

We might spend so much time and energy judging a situation that we no longer focus on the person behind the illness. When we are uncomfortable, it's often apparent by the awkward moments that arise. The awkwardness may come as much from what you don't say, as much as from what you do say. Sometimes, the important thing about communication is to hear what isn't being said. Of course, sometimes words are not necessary; just being present and holding their hand as you watch television together might be enough.

People often don't know what to say to someone who is seriously ill because they spend no time preparing or thinking about it.

If you would like to minimize awkward and uncomfortable moments, it may help to try and organize your thoughts before your visits. Prepare. Think ahead about things you might want to say or do when you are together. It may even help to make a list of the things you want to ask or talk about. Keep in mind the kinds of things they are interested in – hobbies, current events, music, family news. Remember, the list might be a bit different than the things that interest you.

Don't be afraid to ask their advice on a topic. Contrary to burdening them, in some cases, it can help make them feel like they still have something to contribute. If they're an expert in a particular area, you might ask their opinion about something you're dealing with. Or even ask them about a recipe. Feel free to be creative. I wouldn't overwhelm them with questions, but a few at the right time might be fun for them. If they show an interest, you can continue; if not, let it go. Doing this might help make them feel they still have something valuable to contribute, even at the most difficult time in their life.

If we treat the seriously ill person like the viable person they are, that can help us connect more deeply. By removing the veil of judgment, we connect with a person's essence, not the passing circumstances of an illness. This means that the focus of our attention shifts from the external drama to the internal person.

It's our place to help and more often than not, we are better helpers when we are being as non-judgmental as we can be. There is more genuineness when we have this sort of attitude. It's a place where compassionate care can flow most freely.

I'll never forget the moment when I came to this realization during my mother's last few days of life. All her limbs had stopped working and she could only move her eyelids. When I looked in her eyes, I was amazed to see the same person I had known all my life. That hadn't changed. Her body parts had just stopped working. Our communication had been reduced to, *"Blink once for 'yes' and twice for 'no'."* Her eyes were always vibrant and loving. She was herself. Her face didn't look the same, her body had transformed into almost nothing but bones and skin, but her beautiful eyes still spoke very well.

It's so easy to get wrapped up in the surface drama of some situations and overlook other important things like the silent, gentle connection of the eyes or the tender affection of two hands touching. Those moments often speak so much more effectively than spoken words.

Truth resides in every human heart,
and one has to search for it there
and to be guided by truth as one sees it.
But no one has the right to coerce
others to act according to his own view of truth.

–Mahatma Gandhi

CHAPTER 7

LISTENING 101

You may be asking yourself many questions. What can I expect? What are they feeling? What can I do? How can I help? Being able to help means first understanding what's happening with the person we are helping. To understand, we have to listen.

Active, empathetic listening plays a powerful and significant role in communicating with the seriously ill. For those of you who took Psych 101, you may remember the term "active listening." This tool has saved many relationships and is definitely one of the most important tools of communication.

Active Listening_- *Repeating back to the person what you hear them saying in different words than they used.*

For example: Someone says, *"I hate going to the doctors office. I just don't understand why they make everyone sit in that waiting room so long."*

Your response could be, *"It's very frustrating isn't it? The message you get is that you are not that important to them – just another number."*

Or someone says, *"I'm just going to take one day at a time and hope for the best! I'm not dead yet!"*

Your response could be, *"I love your attitude!"* or *"That's great! I feel it too!"* or *"It sounds like you're feeling positive and hopeful."*

Another basic listening skill is looking someone in the eye, and listening as if they are the only person in the world. This sort of focus takes time to develop but it will pay off in the end. Don't let your mind wander when you are with an ill person. Even though it may be boring, be aware that their life is little more than the four walls around them. Be present in the moment. Engage them in conversation, although at times, depending on their energy level, it may not be appropriate, so you'll have to play it by ear. They may want to be alone or be quiet, instead of talking. Or they may be lonely and want to talk. Make sure you always ask if they'd like some time alone, give them the option.

Some people are more eager to offer their stories, their opinions, and their advice, rather than listen to someone else's story. Being a helper means listening at all times and getting involved in someone else's world, and not focusing on your own world. Leave your problems at the front door, and pick them up on your way out. Some people who are ill enjoy getting to know those people around them on a deeper level. If this is the case in your situation, answer all their questions completely and with enthusiasm.

Part of this skill is also to show that you are listening by occasionally using small response words such as: *"hmm," "uh-huh," "OK," "right," or "interesting."* It may seem like a small thing to do, but it makes all the difference in a conversation. The person speaking knows you are with them and that you are present. They know you are listening. They know you care.

PRACTICE LISTENING

Listening skills are exactly that – skills. This infers that they can be learned, practiced and improved. Good listeners are not born, they are developed. One thing I always do when I begin to meditate is to close my eyes, pause and listen to whatever is there. Completely opening myself to whatever is present. Corny perhaps, but I got the idea from a TV show called "Kung Fu." Some of you may recall that show. The master would say to Grasshopper: *"Close your eyes and tell me what you hear."*

When you close your eyes, you invariably become aware of things that you were not conscious of: a plane flying over, a bird singing outside, a squeaky hinge on a door, or even the pulsing of your own heartbeat.

ASSIGNMENT:

Take 5 minutes to practice listening to things that are obvious and yet hidden. Close your eyes and hear what is there.

Practice this listening assignment even a few minutes a day, perhaps in the morning before getting out of bed or at the office. Eventually, you will begin to listen to people in the same way. Not the eyes closed part, of course, but you will hear what is obvious and yet hidden, in them.

Hidden things are buried in someone's tone of voice. If you also pay attention to their body language, eyes and gestures you will learn more about what the seriously ill person is really saying, beyond the words. Silent communication goes on constantly and it reveals the true state of our inner world. Practice observing and waiting for the obvious and the hidden to come to you. Focus and listen. These skills will help you not only with the sick and suffering, but also in your everyday relationships for the rest of your life.

Another reason listening is crucial, is that it makes people feel important. Communication is a great skill to regularly work on because it helps us in all our relationships, whether they are professional or personal.

GETTING PEOPLE TO TALK

It is possible to use empathetic listening as a way to help draw people out. In a friendly way, ask open-ended questions to see if they feel like talking.

What's on your mind today?
Do you feel like talking about what you are going through?
What is the most frustrating thing for you right now?

Tell me more about the last doctor's visit.

While these questions are often avoided, especially if you are uncomfortable or unsure about death, they are all great conversation starters and could lead to a great conversation. (Check Appendix A for more helpful questions.)

Illness is a very lonely road. Anyone who is ill appreciates the attempt at connecting in a place that is real, loving and from the heart. This sort of honest connection is comforting when you are scared and lonely. Let them talk about and cry over the losses they are experiencing. It's counter-productive to say, *"Don't cry. It's going to be all right."* Let them get it out. Sometimes all that is needed is a listening ear and a caring heart.

"It is one of the beautiful compensations in this life that no-one can sincerely try to help another without helping themselves."

– Ralph Waldo Emerson

EIGHT
COMMUNICATION IDEAS

These ideas are excellent points to be aware of to improve communication in any relationship.

FIRST:

Avoid rushing in with advice when someone is sharing.

Give people the space and sufficient time to vent or talk through their emotions. As psychologists tell us, by expressing themselves, people often create their own solutions to their problems. Sometimes we just need someone to listen and as we talk, we find our own way. As they used to say in the monastery, *"God gave us one mouth and two ears. So, listen twice as much as you speak."*

SECOND

Don't pretend to listen when you're not listening.

If you get distracted or go into a daydream while someone is talking, apologize and ask him or her to repeat what they have said. The sincerity you show in wanting to hear what has been said will be appreciated. Again, try to be present to exactly what is going on in the moment.

THIRD

Don't be in the future of a conversation.

This means not mentally preparing your response while the other person is speaking. Just listen. Don't be distracted by thinking you have to control the conversation or add *anything* to it. Just let it flow. Enter into that moment as a relaxed, loving presence. Nothing else.

FOURTH

Be a patient listener.

Sometimes the seriously ill can go on and on (and on) about the most boring topics, and often they repeat themselves. If this happens, be present with them and try to show that you enjoy being with them, regardless of what they want to talk about.

FIFTH

Put down papers, glasses, pamphlets, pens, books, etc.

Playing with these things will give someone the impression that you aren't really interested in them or that you are bored because they are not interesting. Be focused and present. Show you are interested in the person in front of you.

SIXTH

Avoid glancing around the room.

As a listener, your body language is very important and looking anywhere but at the person speaking, communicates that you are restless and bored. Show your interest in the conversation by using open body language. Lean forward when sitting. Avoid crossing your arms, which is an almost universal symbol of skepticism and having a closed mind.

SEVENTH

Be patient as you try to keep the conversation moving.

Without putting them through an inquisition, try asking brief and relevant questions regularly and be sure to wait for a complete answer before asking another question. Sometimes people that are ill talk slowly or ramble on; it can be difficult for them to talk fast and stay focused, especially if they're on certain medications. There may be as much as 30 seconds of silence between question and answer. It takes patience. Most people become uncomfortable with this silence and jump in with another question before the patient has had time to give an answer. In many cases, the patient is not thinking of the answer during that silent time, but they are looking for the energy to speak their words. Remember, it's hard to talk when you are very sick. Consider that the ill person has several drugs in their system, a disease process going on, stress on so many levels and sometimes a good dose of depression.

People who are ill sometimes also lose track of what they were talking about. By making a brief recap statement of what they were saying, you can help them get back on track. If it appears that they are stumbling and have lost their train of thought, you can say something brief to bring them back to the conversation. For example, *"So it sounds like you had a good time with your children this weekend. That's great! What are some other things you did with them?"* or *"And what happened after you went to the store?"*

EIGHTH

Be sensitive to how physically close or far you are from the patient

More often than not they will appreciate closeness, but it's important that we be sensitive that this may change as their need for detachment grows. Whether it's because of moodiness or upbringing, some people just need their personal space more than others. Different cultures dictate different traditions in this respect as well. Always ask before you move in too close.

As much as possible, a helper's job is to present things to the ill person for them to make a decision on. For example, "Would you like to take your pills from a pill cup or have them placed in your hand? Do you want your water with ice or at room temperature?" These sorts of comments may seem simple, but to someone who is ill the consideration will be appreciated.

CHAPTER 9

SPECIAL SKILLS FOR THE CARETAKER

You may have already noticed that many of the things mentioned about communication with the seriously ill are relevant for *all* our relationships. Of course, communication is a cornerstone for success in every personal and business endeavor. There are some communication skills, however, that are especially important to emphasize when being with those who are seriously ill.

PHYSICAL HELP

It is very important to remember that a seriously ill person has been robbed of so many things that we healthy folks take for granted. These things include taking care of personal hygiene, being able to drive, walk, shop alone, or even dial a telephone. The gradual and steep loss of independence is a big blow to most people.

For the person who is very ill, yet still mentally active, so many things are out of their control. They feel like the same person inside, yet their body is falling apart. Because of this they often seek to gain control over the smallest things in their world.

YOUR PART

It can't be overstated how important it is for the ill person to be included in the decision making process of anything that effects their life. These can be difficult conversations.

Commit yourself to being sensitive to this very basic need of your loved one. At the same time, be prepared to know that if a disease progresses, they may not be able to be part of some decisions for their life. It's a tough balancing act. But it's better to err on the side of respect and always try to include them in decisions that will ultimately affect their life.

When my father was ill and confined to a bed, we would sometimes watch TV together. I would chuckle to myself when he would always tell me exactly where to place the remote control after changing the channel. He wanted it precisely on the corner of the table at a 45-degree angle. If I got it wrong, he would let me know every time!

It would have been easy to get irritated by his micromanaging, but when I took a moment and realized that he was compensating, seeking balance, during a time when so much was way out of balance, I was much more understanding, sympathetic, and patient.

BUSINESS DECISIONS

Putting our affairs in order is a very important part of the letting go process. If someone chooses not to do it, that is his or her choice. But by preparing and taking care of the details in advance, the dying person may be helping the family by making sure there is less for them to worry about and organize at the end.

YOUR PART

I think it's important to offer assistance in any way the seriously ill person may need it. If you can do it tactfully, you may do a great service by initiating conversations about their final wishes. This becomes even more helpful if a family tends to be argumentative and self-absorbed (as it becomes more likely that there may be fighting and strife over even the smallest issues that have been left undone by the ill person). I have seen families fight over what songs to sing at a service, or if there would even be a service at all.

Giving an ill person as much control over things as possible lets them feel that they are still worthwhile. This includes appointments to be made with doctors, who will visit, what mail should be looked at or thrown out, and final arrangements.

As much as possible, a helper's job is to present things to the ill person for them to make a decision. For example, *"Would you like to take your pills from a pill cup or have them placed in your hand? What time would you like lunch? Would you like visitors in the morning or later in the afternoon?"*

Constantly presenting options will help them feel better about their life. Always try giving as many options as possible, no matter how small the decision may seem to you. In most cases they will appreciate it and though they may not acknowledge it, it will help them feel as if they still have some control in their own life. Remember: fighting this disease is their full time job. They live constantly reminded of the struggle they are in. Making mundane decisions – like ice or no ice – can help distract them from the intensity of this battle.

DETACHMENT

Obviously, if the dying process is in its final stages it will be harder to keep them in the loop of daily decisions that have to be made. If the disease progresses, they may begin to detach from relationships and material concerns. They may tell you in one way or another they are ready to let go and relinquish these decisions to someone else.

YOUR PART

Be flexible. Keep in mind that there may come a time when their energy returns and they may be able to retake control over decisions that affect them. There is no clear line. Detachment won't necessarily come in specific stages, but often in a frustrating circular spiral. Towards the end, the patient usually comes in and out of being present, in and out of having energy. But with each return, it often seems the intensity of their detachment is increased little by little. Little by little they care less and less.

SPEAKING YOUR PART

Remember to speak gently and in a normal voice when talking to an ill person. So many people speak too loudly, as if the person can't hear. There is no need to yell or speak loudly.

The yo-yo roller coaster tendency of some diseases can really drain the life out of everyone involved. Remember to take time for yourself and review your Comfort Plan to help with patience and understanding during difficult times. The better you take care of yourself, the better you'll be able to care for the ill person.

Night Prayer:
May I be treated tomorrow
the way I treated others today.

CHAPTER 10

CLICHÉS AND TOUGH QUESTIONS

Part of the challenge of being with an ill person is that it often brings up our own unresolved end-of-life issues. When this happens we may become uncomfortable and this is usually when our foot gets directly inserted into our mouth.

Here are five of the most insensitive things I've either said myself or heard others say that are particularly unhelpful to an ill person:

> *Hi, you look great!*
> *So, how are you?*
> *Don't cry.*
> *Be strong!*
> *Don't worry. Cheer up, everything will be fine.*

In this context, clichés are those empty and meaningless things we say to someone when we are unsure of what to say, usually in an effort to lessen our own discomfort around issues of illness or death. Although some of these clichés are not intentionally hurtful or shallow from our perspective, looking at them through the ill person's eyes may make you feel differently. Let's look at them individually.

"Hey, you look great!"

When someone has lost (or gained) a lot of weight, lost their hair, or lost muscle tone, etc., telling them they look great when they obviously do not only comes off as disingenuous, dishonest and detached – and the ill person will know you're not being forthright. Being with a seriously ill person is one of the most real experiences we can ever have. And because it's one of the most real experiences, the more real you are with them, the more connected you will be to their experience. And the more connected you are, the more you'll find yourself in a position to be helpful.

"So, how are you?"

One of the most automatic – and mindless – questions we ask the people around us all day, every day, is how they are; most of the time we don't really expect or even wait for a real answer. But when we're talking with a person who is seriously ill, it's important to be a little more thoughtful about our words and questions.

Once I was visiting a friend who had cancer, and she was not in the greatest of moods that day. Someone stopped by while I was there, and the person asked that classic, mindless question: *"How are you?"* And my friend looked at the questioner without pausing and said, *"I've got cancer, how are you?"* Asking an ill person how they are is probably not the best way to start a conversation; the answer is usually all-too self-evident.

Instead of asking questions, you might make statements that will more naturally lead to conversation. "I've been thinking about you! It's so great to see you." You might also start a conversation with a compliment about something, if you actually have something to really compliment.

"Don't Cry"

When a seriously ill person begins to cry, often someone will jump up and hug them and tell them not to.

Although hearing someone else's tears can make us feel uncomfortable, tears can be a very healthy thing for a person to express. Let someone cry, if they feel like crying! Let them let it out!

The release of the emotion – and the attending tears – can be cathartic and very helpful for the ill person to express. Some say tears are the silent language of the heart.

If you're the one jumping up to tell them not to cry, you might ask yourself why the tears make you so uncomfortable; what exactly makes you feel this discomfort when someone cries; and why do you stifle your own tears? Did you learn this from someone? Answering these questions honestly can be an important step in overcoming some of the fear.

If you're not the one who jumps up and says *"don't cry,"* but you know someone who is, you may want to suggest they read this chapter, if not the whole book. But even if they never see this book, the next time you see them jump into "action," you might take them aside and gently offer some suggestions along the lines of: *"I think it's a good idea for her to cry. It may help her feel better."* Or, *"He's sad that he may be leaving us, and if he cries, it allows him to express this. I think that's a good thing."* Most "don't cry" people don't even realize what they're doing, and once it's pointed out, they tend to stop doing it.

Instead of saying *"don't cry"* you could say: *"It's OK, let your feelings out,"* or *"I'm here to help in any way I can,"* or *"Go ahead and cry – I'm here with you and I love you so much."*

"Be Strong"

Perhaps in an effort to encourage someone, or to be a kind of cheerleader, this misspoken phrase is not helpful to a seriously ill person. Instead, one alternative you might try saying is: *"I know you've got a lot on your plate right now, and if there's anything I can do to help – anything – let me know."* Your offer to be of service, and the love with which you do it, really have meaning for the ill person, so much more than an empty phrase like *"be strong."*

"Don't worry, cheer up. Everything will be fine."

It's when we're most uncomfortable in a situation that we're apt to say unhelpful clichés and other phrases we haven't really thought through. And it's a real disservice to the people we want to help when we do this. If we're not coming from a place of genuineness and honesty, and working toward a more real and deeper connection with the ill person, we come across as trite and insincere. People who are ill need the people around them to be in the present moment and be real. In the words of one friend in his final days: "*I don't have time for b.s.*" He was right and he appreciated it most when people avoided meaningless "happy" phrases in favor of being genuine. Being authentic communicates a sense of love that artificiality can never express.

One day I was visiting a friend newly diagnosed with a serious life threatening illness. She looked at me square in the eyes and said in a tone of fear and desperation: "*Dillon, I'm not going to die, am I?*" Without missing a beat, I was able to match her gaze and said, "*Jane, I don't know what the future holds. But I know that you are surrounded by many people who love you. And, whatever happens, we are all going to get through this together. You will not be alone.*" I must admit that I was surprised at that answer coming out of me so spontaneously. I had no idea, at the time, where it came from. I know now that it came from a place of calm, care and sincerity rather than fear and anxiety.

When we go into a situation with an inner sense of humility, generosity of spirit, and care, we feel a sense of empowerment and ease. When we are in this centered, calm place, it is easier to find good answers to tough questions.

SOME THINGS TO SAY IN PLACE OF CLICHÉS:

- *Could I be one of your "vice presidents in charge of recreation?"*
- *Do you feel like getting out more? Let's do something together.*
- *It's nice to see you again!*
- *Do you feel like talking about what you are going through?*
- *Which family members are you worried about most?*
- *Is there anything special you are craving these days?*
- *What is the most frustrating thing about your life right now?*

Again, focus on being a listener, a helper. Caring for someone who is seriously ill puts you in a very important position. So many spiritual traditions speak of the power of someone being a servant, a power in living a life that helps others.

Remember, if you do make mistakes in communicating with your loved one, you must forgive yourself; learn from the lesson and move on. Of course, we are all going to make mistakes now and then, that's a given. But the important part of the mistake has to do with what we've learned from it. If you've said something you regretted or used one of the clichés we've talked about, take the opportunity to apologize to the ill person for the thoughtless comment. *"I'm sorry I told you not to cry – that was insensitive of me. I'm here for you and you have a shoulder anytime you want it."* Let your loved one know you're sorry, tell them – I guarantee it will open up a more real conversation than you ever imagined. This will help them – and it will help transform you into a more "real" caretaker.

*"Grant me the serenity to accept
the things I cannot change,
Courage to change the things I can,
and the wisdom to know the difference."*
– Anonymous

CHAPTER 11

TALKING IN THE THIRD PERSON AND WHISPERING

Another common mistake people make, and by this I mean many people, including doctors, nurses and social workers, is that they talk about the seriously ill person in their presence in the third person. When do you ever do that with an adult? Someone becomes very ill and suddenly it's as though they are not there at all.

I was once working with an oncologist on a case, over a period of 14 months, and I noticed a shift in the way the doctor would talk to the patient. As the cancer progressed, the doctor began to talk *about* the patient and not to the patient. When I noticed this was becoming a habit, I pulled the doctor aside and pointed it out to her. She was shocked to realize that she had slipped into doing such a thing, but it's easy to see how it could happen. On this point we all need to be careful and aware if it happens.

Remember that there is a person in front of you, and that this person, even if bedridden, is listening and aware. Most ill people appreciate being brought into every conversation that relates to him or her. It is their life! They're not dead. If at all possible, do not exclude them from conversations about their life.

For example, instead of saying, *"He's doing very well today and his right side is a lot stronger than it was yesterday."* Try something like this, *"I think Sam would agree that the right side is much stronger than yesterday. How do you feel about that Sam, do you think that's true?"* Never use the third person in the presence of the seriously ill person! It can be a very subtle, hurtful and demeaning experience at this time in life. What many ill people think to themselves is, *"Why isn't he talking to me? What's the matter, don't I exist anymore?"*

These are the questions that pass through the mind of a seriously ill person who is struggling to accept their situation. As if things weren't hard enough, now they get to listen to people talk about them as if they weren't even there. What a lonely experience that must be.

WHISPERING

If you feel you have to whisper, then you are too close. Go outside, go into another room, close the door, and leave the area. Do anything you need to do to get out of whisper mode. The seriously ill person hears very well and in many cases better than ever.

Whispering communicates secrecy and does not encourage trust and openness. When you realize that you are dying there can be moments that are very scary and most people feel incredibly alone. When you are ill the only things that really bring a sense of inner peace are feelings of love, trust and care. That's why, more than ever, you need loving, trusting and caring people around you. This is what brings comfort to someone who is seriously ill. People who whisper are not being a comfort or a support.

When you whisper the ill person will ask themselves many questions, like *"Why are they whispering? What don't they want me to know? What are they hiding from me?"* Then fear sets in and this may contribute to their shutting down emotionally, in the same way speaking to them in the third person would. Whispering is counterproductive.

CHAPTER 12

ANGER

There are times when the ill person will explode with venomous anger directed at whoever is close. This sometimes alienates the ill person even more because the loved ones take it personally, become resentful, and stop visiting or calling. Although this reaction is common, and even somewhat natural, it's helpful to understand that anger is an important part of the ill person's coming to terms with the situation they're in. This anger may be caused by a combination of things: lack of sleep, fear, medications, and all the various frustrations involved with their reality.

On several occasions, I've noticed that some ill people are too nice to dish out anger at the people around them. So, they lash out at generic things like garbage trucks, "*I hate those damn trucks, they're too loud.*" Or the post office, "*I wish that damn post office would get their delivery schedule straight.*"

Their world becomes very focused on their sickness and they can become self-absorbed, short-tempered, and maybe unappreciative. It's not that they are truly ungrateful, but they may forget to say thank you and show common gestures of gratitude to those around them. Some people who are ill have moments when they become overly demanding and rude. They may insist that others serve and do things for them – this is just another expression of anger. Their actions scream, "*I deserve special treatment.*" This can be difficult to be around. Even after spending just a little time with them, you can leave emotionally exhausted.

WHEN LOSING A MOTHER OR FATHER

Genuine anger or cross words coming from a parent can be a painful experience. Sometimes a terminal disease, dementia, or stroke can change the personality of a loved one. Sometimes it changes for the better, sometimes for the worse. Don't take it personally if you find that your ill parent becomes angry, short tempered, or hostile. It's not your fault! Do your best to remind yourself that it's the disease process at work.

Also remember that some parents try to protect their children. This is especially true with a family that has young children. If the parent tries to hide details of the illness from you, it can't be taken personally. It's possible they want to keep you from feeling any distress, burden or pain. Don't take it as rejection or feel overly hurt if this happens. Chances are, this is their effort to look after you, and though it may not seem that way at the time, a way of expressing love toward you. They may only be doing what is natural for them as a parent – protecting their child.

Still other parents have a whole different approach to their dying process. I recently spoke to a woman who had been at death's door because of cancer (it eventually went into remission). She says that she saw her death as a part of life – not separate from it. She wanted her kids to be close through the entire process. So, she had private talks with each family member. She told me, *"I had to be sure everyone was OK with my approaching death. I had things I wanted say. They needed to be prepared to let go and move on. I wanted to make sure there was nothing left unsaid. I saw this as a part of my parenting duty."*

CHAPTER 13

DEPRESSION AND SLEEP

As the disease progresses, sleeping may take a more a prominent place in the daily schedule. It is a common experience that the ill person spends an increasing amount of time in deeper and deeper sleep. They may appear to be uncommunicative, unresponsive, or difficult to awaken. This is normal, due in part to a change in their metabolism, perhaps to the kinds of drugs they are on or to the emotional need for detachment. They may also be less concerned with eye contact, as a way of detaching from those around them. During this time, it is important for the helper to be present by just sitting quietly and maybe holding their hand.

Don't take offense if a person who is ill pulls away from you when you attempt to reach out to them. If they pull their hand away from yours or refuse a foot massage, maybe they would like to be alone. Ask them. For some, it is a common experience to want quiet time for rest and meditation. Some people need a lot of alone time. Some need space to detach themselves from their surroundings. Don't take it personally if they don't seem to want you around.

They might withdraw and care less about their appearance, and may also want to bathe less. Anyone who occasionally struggles with depression will recognize this as a typical feeling. To not care what you look like or smell like; to not care if your hair is clean or dirty; to just not care about anything at all is quite typical of depression. Everything basic to your existence becomes an effort. A large part of you just wants to be left alone. You don't have the energy it takes to interact with others.

On the other hand, it is sometimes common for seriously ill people to try and avoid sleep. In this case, they often don't want to sleep because they are afraid that they will never wake up and they don't want to miss anything.

Sleep in the early part of a disease is sometimes different from sleep in the later part of a disease. In the early stages of a disease, sleep brings genuine rest. Like healthy folks, they wake up refreshed, though this feeling of refreshment may not last as long as it did when they were healthy.

Sleep in the middle stages of a disease, may be inconsistent and never restful. They may never really wake up feeling refreshed and may always feel worn down. The patient wakes up feeling tired and may remain tired all day.

In the very last weeks of someone's life, it is common that the ill person enter into a deep, coma like sleep. They may awaken now and then to drink or talk. But soon they drift back off to a deep sleep. It's possible that the purpose of deep sleep, at this level, is to help the ill person slowly detach from their surroundings.

Detachment is an important part of the dying process. Some spiritual traditions say that as the dying process evolves, our internal energy (internal dimension or spirit) is preparing for a departure from the physical body and the physical world. In India it is called "dropping the body." The basis for this thought is that we are spiritual beings with a physical dimension – not a physical being with a spiritual dimension. So, the body is dropped by the spirit. This tradition says that the spirit lives on.

But, before it moves on, sleep plays an important role in breaking the attachments that we all have nurtured in our lives – attachments to people, attachments to roles that we have held in family or society, and attachments to work that was ours to do while we were here. In the end, we must let go of it all. Sleep seems to gently help us do this.

There are many hospice workers with stories that illustrate the need for some people to be alone at the time of their death. Sometimes if a loved one seems to be hanging on and not letting go, it could be because they're bothered by family members too much! People often think they are doing a good thing by trying to engage them in conversation or activity. *"Wake up, Aunt Helen, it's me Julie." Julie, leave her alone! Let her sleep if she's tired.*

It's common for a dying person to wait until they are completely alone before they let go and cross over. There are many stories of people who kept a constant vigil at the bedside, only to find that in that one moment when they slipped away to use the restroom, or to grab something to eat, their loved one had died. It seems many people need a private moment to be alone, to "drop the body."

I remember visiting an elderly, grief-stricken wife who tried to awaken her failing husband, by yelling (in a thick Polish accent), *"Honey, wake up,"* she said lightly tapping his face. *"Would you like something to drink? Honey, wake up. Look, this nice young man came here to see us. He wants to know if we need anything."*

Then after a long pause, she looked at me with very sad eyes and said, *"Oh, I don't know what's happening. Sometimes I try to wake him and he just won't wake up."*

She needed help in accepting his impending death. She was beside herself in grief, shock and confusion. In our short time together she kept saying one thing over and over: *"Sixty-four years together. What am I going to do?"*

I remember being struck with sadness, yet also inspiration at such a beautiful life they had together. She told me about their years of glory. How they met as teenagers and fled Poland and arrived in New York. She pulled out pictures. He had been a tailor and she opened her closets and proudly showed all the clothes he had made her. I wasn't sure at all what I should say or do. So, I just listened and let her talk. When in doubt, listening is always safe.

CHAPTER 14

WHAT IS
"DYING WITH DIGNITY"?

To a large extent, dying with dignity can be considered a mythical concept. Technically, keeping an ill person clean and free of pain is not only important, but it does allow them to die with some level of dignity. However, watching someone's humanity slowly disintegrate, is one of the most difficult experiences a caretaker can have. Often times, especially when feeling overwhelmed, it makes the ability to see any dignity at all incredibly difficult.

I wonder if what we are searching for is not "dying with dignity," but surviving with dignity. The ill person has many thoughts, emotions and fears to come to terms with. Sometimes it is the surviving friends and family members who are the ones preoccupied with seeking dignity. They want to remember the ill person in their healthy state: clean, esthetically pleasing, of sound mind, etc. This is not bad. But, maybe what we should be most concerned with is *depth* in dignity.

With depth of dignity comes intimacy, deep compassion and caring. On the deepest level within us, feelings about dignity are closely tied to intimacy and caring. I have been lucky to witness, on several occasions, the spouse who cares for a partner as if the two of them are one person. It is inspirational to watch this kind of love in action. To walk every step with someone in "the valley of the shadow of death" is a very intimate and selfless act. The spouse or loved one who feels inspired to walk this journey, in order to help tend to the many details, is fortunate indeed. They will never be the same. This sort of work changes a life in so many positive ways.

However, be forewarned: exhaustion, high stress and burnout are all common experiences in the lives of those who, day-in and day-out hold the hand of someone who is ill. If death approaches, even strong people can crumble under the torments a deathwatch can bring. It is especially difficult if the ill person is someone you love and have history with. Most who walk every step of this journey as a companion to the ill person, find the way long and some days the sun beats down, unbearably hot. At times like these, it is a good idea to refer to your Comfort Plan to help remind you of your own needs and what brings you comfort to relieve some of your stress.

When someone has a terminal disease, it can drain them of vitality, and slowly take away his or her life energy. Every life is unique and this uniqueness extends to the way we die; so often, we die the way we live. This means the coping skills we developed in life to deal with a crisis will be the coping skills we use to deal with serious illness.

CREATING A COMFORTABLE ENVIRONMENT

There are some small things that you can do for a seriously ill person to make their life run more smoothly. Purchase a wireless doorbell ($20.00) at an electronic store. This gadget is immensely helpful for the ill person when they are in bed and need assistance. By simply pressing a button help is on the way. An old fashioned bell by the bedside also works. But, pressing a button is much easier when you are sick and your energy is low. You could also use a wireless baby monitor.

Also, a cassette player near the bed, with a few meditation or music tapes within reach, is helpful. Should your loved one wake in the middle of the night, it is important that they have something nearby to help occupy their mind and time. Watching TV can also help pass the time. But meditation tapes not only occupy their time, they can also help facilitate a feeling of being focused, centered and encouraged. I once knew a woman who received a gift: a tape by her friends where they all took turns reading their favorite inspirational pieces. Some read a Bible passage, some read a poem, some just spoke calming words of love and support. It was a great gift in those lonely moments. (Check out Appendix B for some meditation tape recommendations.)

EYE CONTACT

Careless practices, like those mentioned previously – talking in the third person, whispering, talking in nearby rooms about them, not letting them make decisions for their life – cuts you off from being able to facilitate a high level of dignity. In the most basic sense of what dignity is, we should do nothing that would stop someone who is ill from wanting to look in our eyes. The eyes are where souls meet. If eye contact is possible, it is a very important thing to have lots of during this last chapter of life. In the end, dignity with depth consists of a lot of heartfelt eye contact, hugs, hand massages, foot rubs, cuddles, and kisses. Words may not even be important or even needed.

NEW MEDICINES

In this new millennium, scientists are hopeful we will find a cure for cancer and every disease known to the human race. I personally know many people whose lives have been extended thanks to new medications and medical technology.

Whatever the disease (Cancer, Heart Disease, Parkinson's, Alzheimer's, AIDS, etc.) medical science is giving us the means by which our lives are being sustained longer with disease. With the onset of these new medicines, death will take most of us a little bit at a time. What has changed is the length of time that we now have to live with disease. We now have more time to tie up loose ends and enjoy moments of life we were too busy to enjoy before. We have time to build bridges in relationships that may have gone astray. This can make all the difference in the world to our peace of mind.

Until they find a cure for whatever disease has taken the body hostage, medicines should be seen for what they are: not a cure, but a gift of a few more months or years to live. Some in this situation find that their quality of life increases because they are forced to live for now, more present to the moment. With this new focus, the gift of more time can help us in all our relationships. We have time to make amends, or do some things we have only dreamed about. It can be a time to do things we have always wanted to do. It's not too late to learn the lessons you were too busy to learn when you were healthy. It's not too late to do the fun things you were too busy to do. And it's not too late to learn what all the fuss is about with all these sunsets!

One day while caught in the moment of a beautiful sunset, a dear friend struggling with cancer said, *"Dillon, the best things in life really are free. My dad would sing that song all the time. I see now, more than ever, it really is true. The best things in life are free."*

CHAPTER 15

TAKING AN INVENTORY

Over the years, I have observed many things as I sat at the bedsides of people who were dying. One thing I especially noticed was the disposition of the person who was dying. For those that I would classify as "peacefully dying" I noticed they were also the people who talked most freely about their life and their feelings. They seemed more at peace with themselves with others and with the environment.

Because of this, they seemed more open to dialogue about things that are more personal in nature. For these people, it became important to talk about special moments of the past. This is part of taking their inventory of attachments and loves. Recalling them can somehow help us to let go, say goodbye. Some people never come to this place, though I think most people do, in one way or another.

Taking an inventory means taking time for reflection, and maybe even having conversations about the past.

As a caretaker or loved one, it's important that you not discourage these kinds of conversations. It may lead to making amends where needed, and maybe even reconciliation with a person or two. I have noticed that an ill person reminisces a lot during the last few months or weeks of life. Walking down memory lane, and telling stories of past successes, fun moments, and even failures, are important steps to take. On one level, I think they are searching for the meaning of their life. They are quietly searching for how they left the world a better place. Searching for an answer to the question: *"What difference did my life make?"*

I can still hear the words my dad said a few days before he died: *"I left four really great kids in the world. I always did basically whatever I wanted to. I had a pretty good life."* I believe his words – and his need for reflection – are true for many people at the end of their life. There comes a time where there is a great need for reflection and inner thought. A need to talk. Encourage these conversations.

QUESTIONING YOURSELF

Growing up in a religious environment, I became accustomed to going on retreats sponsored by our church. I always enjoyed retreats – even as a rebellious teenager – because they gave me the opportunity to connect, in a deeper way, with other kids my age. I had only been to a few retreats when I decided I wanted to help lead them. As I gained this leadership experience, I began to see retreats as an opportunity to question myself and reflect on my own life experiences. I would always use at least some of the retreat time to do a sort of self-evaluation. I began a collection of questions and exercises, which I sometimes still use (see Appendix A for samples). Every year around December 30, I write out the answers to questions like these in my journal. Reflecting on the past year, and dreaming about the coming year are ways that I get to know myself, what I value and where I'm going. Also, it's interesting every year to read what I wrote the year before.

Self knowledge can carry with it a feeling of empowerment. Luckily, you can get to know yourself in many ways. But, one easy way is to simply ask yourself a few soul searching questions. It's part of creating a conscious relationship with yourself. If it's not the kind of thing you have given much thought to or if you have been putting off some self-reflection, try using the questions at the end of this chapter as a starting place. Don't wait for the end of your life to start working on the skills of reflection. I've observed that the people who really took time to get to know themselves (people who had an inner security) had the most inner peace in the last chapter of life. As a caretaker, maybe some self-reflection can bring you that sense of empowerment and peace now.

You may also want to present some of these questions to your ill friend, if you feel it would be appropriate, and, of course, only if they seem open to the idea. In some cases, a conversation is easier than having them write their answers out. However, getting their answers in writing can be a nice memento for a spouse or child to have. In journals we leave a bit of ourselves behind.

I once bought a blank journal at a bookstore and wrote a question at the top of every fifth page. I then gave it to a friend who was in a battle with cancer. After she went through it, she told me how appreciative she was for having it and she let me read it. I was very happy I had followed through on the idea. It really helped her process the many feelings she was having, and it started a meaningful conversation with one of her children. Feeling connected to someone important in her life enabled her to take one more step toward closure.

ALONE TIME

Another part of inventory is being alone. Some people live their lives so that they are never alone. All relationships take time and effort, and our relationship with our self is no exception. It has been my observation that in the end, a person who is uncomfortable being alone has more stress at this point in life. The intense feeling of fear, which is often seen as fear of death, is sometimes nothing more than a fear of being alone. Many healthy people, people who still have years of life ahead of them, fear being alone.

If the ill person you are with is someone who is afraid of being alone, they would most certainly benefit from frequent attention and affection. Someone being in the room with them, watching TV or even just reading silently, is an easy thing to coordinate in shifts. Get as many loved ones involved as possible. If there aren't enough family members or friends, call a local hospice organization, and you'll undoubtedly meet some of the coolest, kindest volunteers in your area.

Take time to think and reflect on what has gone on in your life. What statement are you making with your life? Think about it now, as opposed to the end of your life. If you think about it now and you don't like the answer you get, you'll have some time to make changes – before it's too late.

ASSIGNMENT

Take some time to write answers out to these self-reflection exercises.

Name a crisis in your life that was very challenging. How did you handle that situation? Explain the details.

What is the most challenging part of your life right now?

List 5-10 of your closest friends (or family members). Then, write a few sentences describing your interactions with them this past year. How do you feel about each person? Describe them, what feelings you have for a each person, and what they contribute or don't contribute to your life.

What did you worry about most this past year?

Write about why you are unique and why the world is a better place because you are in it.

What made you laugh hard over the past year?

Describe your dreams for each of your children or grandchildren (if you don't have children, describe your dreams for a significant person in your life).

For me, family means: (list 7 things)

Name two things you have learned about life in the last couple of years.

List all the things from this past year for which you feel grateful.

Write your own epitaph, as it would read today.

If you could add an eleventh commandment what would it say?

CHAPTER 16

SEX, AFFECTION AND TOUCH

The need for affection and for sex varies in all of us. The mechanisms that drive these desires are as individual as we are. Not only do these mechanisms vary among individual personalities, but the need for affection or sex will sometimes change and evolve with the stages of life. Overall, however most people who are sick for long periods of time don't often feel very sexy – or sexual.

I have known a few seriously ill people who were still interested in sex while they were sick, although that seems to account for a fairly small percentage. It would also seem for the vast majority of those who are ill, affection, more than sex, is appreciated and important.

For the most part, affection and nurturing is what many people, healthy and unhealthy, long for. Touching, hugging, handholding, and kisses on the forehead are all incredibly comforting to many of us when we are ill. A foot rub never felt so good or meant so much. Manicures and hand massages have never been so appreciated!

When my mother was in her last few days, she was mostly in a coma. She was always a very affectionate mother and loved holding hands and getting a little foot massage. One day I walked into my parent's apartment to find my brother cuddled up with my mom in her bed. He was just lying there, holding her like she must have done with us when we were on the other end of the life cycle. She lay there in the fetal position as if she were a dear, tender child. Even though she could not talk to us at that time, I'm sure she loved being held. Seeing my brother and mother wrapped in such tender affection stands as one of the beautiful memories of my life.

Affection is clearly something important to most of the ill people I have been with, but I do not want to give the impression that in the end all people are affectionate. I'm sure there are some people who have never liked being touched and continue disliking it to the end. Either way, I think it is always important to be sensitive to cultural differences in personal space, touching, and even handshakes.

In some places of the world, direct eye contact is considered disrespectful, hugs are only initiated by the eldest person and personal contact – kissing a cheek for example – is completely taboo, while in other countries it's perfectly customary and welcomed. When walking into a new situation, be conservative and let them guide you; you'll know soon enough what their customs and boundaries are.

A SAFE BET

If you want physical contact but are unsure if the ill person will be accepting, a safe place to touch them would be the forearm, between the elbow and the wrist.

What is it to die but to stand naked in the wind and to melt into the sun? And what is it to cease breathing, but to free the breath from its restless tides, that it may rise and expand and seek God unencumbered?

- Kahlil Gibran

CHAPTER 17

WHEN THE END IS NEAR

It's impossible to know exactly the day or time when someone will pass. However, there are definitely signs of life energy leaving the body.

PHYSICAL SIGNS

In Tibet they look at dying as a slow disconnection from the elements of earth, water, fire, and air.

Earth
- Patient becomes weak.
- The body may become heavy and unable to carry itself.
- The body begins to settle down toward the earth to which it will return.
- Earth element leaves the body.

Water
- Patient becomes thirsty. Skin and mouth become dry.
- Water element leaves the body.

Fire
- Patient asks for sweater or extra blankets.
- Hands and feet may be cool to the touch.

    • The body becomes frequently cold.
    • Fire element leaves the body.

Air
    • The in-breath becomes shorter than the out-breath.
    • Air element leaves the body.

ADDITIONAL SIGNS

Disorientation
    • The person gets confused as to where they are, or what time it is.

Incontinence
    • The bladder and rectal muscles begin to relax and let go.

Restlessness
    • They may appear to make uncontrollable, restless, and repetitive motions such as pulling at clothing or wiping a spot on a table.

Appetite Decreases
    • It's common for cravings and appetite to come and go. Do not force food or manipulate them into eating. If they don't have an appetite, don't constantly remind them of this fact. If nausea is a problem, ask the doctor to order a medication that will take care of it.

Withdrawal
    • They may seem very aloof and detached from their surroundings.

Congestion
    • A constant gurgling sound is heard when they breathe.
    • This is sometimes called a "death rattle."
Also, towards the end of our lives dizziness and fainting may worsen. Sleeping will be frequent and may at times appear coma like. The ill person will look older, act weaker and will tire more easily. Every step becomes a chore, their memory becomes worse, handwriting is less legible and an overall zest for life (their life energy) fades. Again, they care less than they used to about earthly matters.

LETTING GO

In the end, some people who are ill won't let go, and they fight to the final breath. Sometimes they don't want to die because they worry about those they will leave behind. On more than one occasion, it has become necessary for family members to go to the dying person one at a time and give them permission to die. Words like, *"we'll be fine"* and *"if it's time for you to go, I'm going to be okay"* can help the dying person let go and make the transition more willingly. By doing this, you encourage them to let go and not feel guilty for leaving. It is common for a dying person to hold on until they are sure those left behind will be OK.

If it gets to this point and there are young children present, be sure to reach out to them on their level. Talk in words that they understand. Don't be afraid to see if they have any questions and answer them as honestly as you can. When someone does go into a coma, don't tell children they are asleep, a child could develop a fear of dying in their sleep. Instead, be honest and say, *"Grandma has cancer and is dying."* Most children cope much better than we do with the issue of death.

*Cuddle in bed with your ill loved one,
or hold their hand and say everything
you need to say. "I just want you to know..."*

CHAPTER 18

NURSING HOMES

A discussion of nursing homes can be an emotional one. It's not uncommon for people to feel guilty for putting their loved one in a home. On the other hand, there are some situations in which putting someone in a home is the best and/or the only option. While this is always a difficult decision, there are many good nursing homes that pay close attention to the people living under their care. But how do you find these good places? What questions do you ask when you visit?

First, call anyone you know who has already gone through the experience of searching for a good nursing home. See if you can learn anything from their experience. Do they have any tips on how to start? What would they do differently if they had to do it again?

Second, you could try a surprise inspection on a nursing home. Just show up and be a fly on the wall. Sit down and read through a magazine for 30 minutes and discretely observe what goes on. If you can, get a seat near the nursing station, where staff members tend to talk. Observe how they talk about the patients. Do they conduct themselves professionally? Are they caring? Do they make fun of patients? Do they seem attentive?

Third, call hospice organizations in your area and ask to speak to a case manager about nursing home recommendations. They will be able to give you exact recommendations based on the specific type of facility you are looking for.

I once had a friend who had the responsibility of putting a loved one in a nursing home. She hit the yellow pages and started calling all the nursing homes listed in her area. An appointment to meet with the administrator of each institution was made.

I asked her how she came to choose the nursing home she eventually decided on. She said, *"Well, I went to six of them and met everyone. They all seemed about the same. I liked a couple of them more than the rest, but there wasn't any significant difference between them. To be honest, I think the biggest factor in my decision for the one I chose was the smell of the place when I walked in. There were green plants around. Everything was clean, people were friendly, and it didn't smell like a nursing home. It smelled good."*

I expected an answer that was a bit more philosophical. But, it makes sense. If you love someone, you want him or her to be in a place that feels and smells clean.

Recently, I received an email from Maria Smith, a nurse with extensive experience in caring for the seriously ill. She wrote, *"when selecting a good nursing facility I would chose the one that has the best pressure sore prevention policy and find out if the policy is actually carried out. This is hard to do but generally goes hand in hand with the smell factor. So many of my nursing friends and I have worked for fraudulent care providers who promise one thing, but do another."*

Consumer Reports Complete Guide to Health Services for Seniors is a terrific resource that helps caregivers negotiate through the health care maze. The book offers hands-on, practical advice in a user-friendly format that includes worksheets, charts and comparative tables designed to help make important long-term care decisions. The guidebook lists two new tools for choosing nursing homes, the "Nursing Home State Detection Index," and the "Nursing Home Watch List by State." For more information, call 800-500-9760 or visit Consumer Reports online at http://www.consumerreports.org.

Here are some other "hands-on" suggestions to help you in your search:

• Some nursing homes open their cafeteria to visitors. If so, have lunch there and see what the food is like.

- Meet the people who run the facility. Ask if you can walk around to get a feel for the place.

- When meeting with them, ask straightforward questions: Have you ever been sited for a violation by the county? Have you ever been sited for being understaffed? Have you ever been sited for food being cooked improperly?

- Is the place clean?

- Do the workers look happy and kind?

- Are workers attentive to and talking to patients or ignoring them?

- What is the ratio of R.N.s / L.P.N.s / Aides per shift, per person?

- What activities are provided?

- Is there a doctor on the premises 24 hours?

- If you see some patient visitors, see if you can speak to them, and ask if they like having their loved one in this particular home. What are their impressions of the place?

- And last, but not least, how does it smell?

It's not morbid to be honest about death.
We come to truly appreciate life here
and now when we see that someday,
we will not have it.

CHAPTER 19

NURSES AND NURSING AGENCIES

When serious illness comes into our lives, many of us won't be able to have a fulltime nurse help us with all the details that need tending to. In most cases, a family member or close friend can learn most of the basic things that need to be done to help a seriously ill person in their many needs.

Being certified in First Aid can help a lot in getting to know basic terminology. If you need any equipment (hospital bed, oxygen tank, etc.) a local hospice can either loan it to you or tell you where you can rent it. Most hospices can also train you in the use of equipment (e.g. how to change an I.V. bag). Don't be shy about calling your local hospice to ask a question about how to care for someone who is seriously ill. If they can't help you, they will be able to point you in the right direction.

In Appendix C, the issue of hiring caretakers is visited in more detail. But in short, if you need to hire someone to assist you, there are several different types of helpers to choose from. Below is a brief overview:

CAREGIVER

Whatever the patient needs done, however they need help, a

caregiver is there to support and aid. Creating a safe environment tops the list of duties. Depending on their skills, they could do everything from laundry to driving errands to balancing the checkbook. They don't usually have a nursing education.

NURSING AIDES

The next kind of help is called an Aide. Nursing Aides are a little more focused on healthcare and issues that surround it. They usually have a certification in basic life support class. They can provide skin care, do vital signs, etc.

L.P.N. (LICENSED PRACTICAL NURSE) OR L.V.N. (LICENSED VOCATIONAL NURSE)

L.P.N.'s (or L.V.N.s) would have a little more nursing education than an Aide does. Basic nursing duties and medical terminology would be within their area of expertise. Dressing changes, signs and symptoms of infection, suctioning, colostomy care, and medications might all fall under their duties. If the nurse (R.N.) is trained to think critically and medically assess a situation, an L.P.N. would be the technician that would assist in carrying out that care.

R.N. (REGISTERED NURSE)

A Registered Nurse, has finished either two or four years of nursing education. These classes would be considered advanced classes in life support and nursing duties. They would be taught to think critically about a case and assess or monitor the care that is given. They are skilled in many tasks. Among them would be skin care, mouth care, exercises to do while in bed, nutrition, respiratory challenges, etc. They are able to attach an I.V. to the patient, and they usually work in conjunction with the doctors on a case. Through hospice, a nurse is usually available on call to guide the family with whatever needs arise.

NURSING AGENCY

If you call a nursing agency, to find nursing help you can expect the agency to send nurses who will know how to provide basic "by-the-book" care. But this is not necessarily optimal care. Not all helpers know how to provide thorough, optimal care. I consider 'optimal care' to be another phrase for "total patient care". By this I mean not just caring for the person's bodily needs, but their emotional, spiritual and psychological needs as well. So, this means you have to screen well. When meeting/interviewing nurses, if you don't like the person who has been sent, call the agency immediately and say, *"Please send me a different nurse."* It's as simple as that. Most agencies realize – and expect – that people may try more than one nurse before they decide on one.

Finally, if you are lucky enough to find good people that work well in your situation, be sure to treat them with genuine appreciation. It's hard to do this work, and you need good, reliable people that work well together. Be sure to take the time to let them know how much their help is appreciated and to thank them. It takes a special person to do this sort of work.

We do not know whether it is good to live or to die.
Therefore, we should not take delight in living
nor should we tremble at the thought of death.
We should be equiminded toward both.
This is the ideal.

- Mohandas K. Gandhi

CHAPTER 20

ORGANIZATIONAL ISSUES

EXPECT THE BEST BUT BE PREPARED FOR THE WORST

There are many issues to be resolved at the end of our life. No matter your age, should the unexpected happen, it is best to be responsible, and at least somewhat prepared. By tending to the details of our affairs we give a gift to those loved ones we leave behind. It is a stressful time for them. The more detailed we are in our instructions, the less there will be for them to stress about and organize. Also, it gives those left behind one more opportunity to show their loyalty and love by carrying out our final wishes. By doing what we ask, they are doing us one, last favor - one last act of love and devotion. But above all, it can help to create more peace in the family at a very stressful time.

With almost all of us, there are basic issues of inheritance and possessions. It doesn't matter if you are worth $5,000 or $5,000,000. If you don't have a will, you are not thinking of the wasted time and expense that your loved ones will have to endure once you are gone. If you don't have a will, state law will decide who gets what, if anything.

As one friend once put it, *"when you die, everything you have is going to be given to charity. It will either be your most favorite charity - your loved ones, a hospital - or your least favorite charity – the government! You decide."*

Even if you think you don't have many material possessions, it's important to consult an attorney who specializes in estate planning. There are so many legal avenues that can be taken to minimize the amount of money going to your least favorite charity. Charitable trusts and other types of legal instruments are what estate attorneys create. Tending to these details before it's too late can do a lot of good. For those who are left behind, it's never too early for this sort of preparation, but it can certainly be too late. After the estate planning is completed, there are smaller, more intimate issues for which an attorney would not be necessary.

These final plans (memorial service, reception, etc.) can be an important thing to talk about. It might be uncomfortable to talk about. But, if you can, it's an important thing to do. Look for a time to talk to the ill person about their wishes. If it feels appropriate, you could even say something like, *"Mom, this is kind of awkward to talk about. But I'm wondering if you have any special requests for us if we come to a place that we have to plan a memorial service. I hope we won't need a service for many, many, many years. But, whenever we do need one, it would be nice to know we did it the way you wanted to."*

One lady I knew once said, *"I want lots of singing!"* And that's exactly what we did.

CHECKLIST

Is a "living will" completed?

If not, ask the doctor for a form and do it right away. This is sometimes called a Healthcare Directive. Have your loved one(s) be clear about what they would like regarding medical care should they not be able to speak for themselves. (We should all have these, by the way. Keep five or six copies in easy to get places. This would include your car glove compartment, in case of an automobile accident; you may want the emergency room to know your wishes, should you not be able to speak for yourself.)

Power of attorney.

Should the patient be in an unresponsive state, someone will need to be able to sign a legal document for them. Usually Power Of Attorney is given to a spouse or family member. You should be aware that there is a difference between a Power of Attorney and a Health Care Power Of Attorney – both vitally important but serve different purposes.

In some states, Power of Attorney may refer to the power someone has to speak for someone else in matters of property, finances, and other issues. Healthcare Power of Attorney is limited only to healthcare and medical decisions that need to be made in that regard.

Why would you want two different people with different types of Power of Attorney? I'll quote a nurse I recently spoke to about this subject. She said, *"I have two different people because if I'm in an unresponsive state and some decisions need to be made about my healthcare, I want someone to make a decision based on what they know I would want done. My husband has Power of Attorney over all our "things." But, we've only been married a few years. I'm not sure he would really know what I would want in a complicated medical situation. So, I gave my sister Healthcare Power of Attorney because I felt she knows me the best."*

Sometimes these healthcare decisions can be very complex. You want someone that knows you well and can think well under pressure, and most importantly, would know what you would want in a given situation.

Arranging Healthcare Directives, Power of Attorney and Healthcare Power of Attorney don't necessarily require the input of an attorney, if money is an issue. There are some terrific do-it-yourself forms and software to be had at relatively little cost. If you went to your local bookstore, you would find, among others, a list of books and forms from Nolo Press, who offer plain-language, legal self-help, often recommended by lawyers themselves. You could also visit their Web site, at www.nolopress.com, and you'd find an overview of estate planning issues in their useful Questions and Answers section. If you're a computer-literate person, software called Quicken Lawyer (available on the Nolo press Web site) offers easy-to-follow forms for everything discussed here, all in one package. You'll also find Quicken Lawyer available in most large bookstores.

Are internment arrangements completely finished?
Consider the following:
- Cremation or burial.
- Name and location of cemetery or where and how you want the ashes to be distributed.
- Where will the service be held? Private or public service?
- 6-8 pallbearers needed. Names and contact information.
- Readings to be arranged. Titles of readings and who will read them, and contact information.
- Name of the Minister, Rabbi, organizer or facilitator of the service.
- Speakers and their contact information.
- Songs you would like sung at this gathering.
- Singer's names and contact information.
- Would your loved one like to write a letter to friends that are gathered or talk on a tape video or audio, that would be played at the service?
- In lieu of flowers, would they like an organization to receive donations? If so, which organizations?
- How would they like the newspaper obituary to read?

Large possessions
- House.
- Bank accounts, trusts, stock/portfolio information, etc.
- Cars, boats, etc.

Smaller possessions
- Rings/jewelry.
- Artwork.

- Stereo/furniture.
- Kitchenware, dishes, silverware, pots and pans.
- Personal hygiene items (razor, blow dryers, etc.).
- Clothing.
- Books.
- Journals / personal videotapes.
- Pictures.
- Awards received.

Letters

An ill person may want to consider writing a letter to those who are especially close and arrange that the notes be given out after the funeral. This is another chance to say things that have been left unsaid. Letters might go to:

- Immediate family members
- Close friends
- Work associates
- People in clubs/boards/societies

Special Gifts From A Parent

Losing a parent is a very difficult thing, especially for young families. It may take years for a young family to bounce back, and find the new rhythm that is created by the loss of one of the parents. It's important to keep regular communication open with young children who have just had a traumatic loss of a parent. They may silently worry about many things. For example, they may wonder if the remaining parent will remarry. The best way to handle it is to talk to the children about what their feelings are. Give them permission to say anything about how they are feeling. This is a great gift to give to a child. Give them tender, individual attention.

People often ask me for ideas of what a parent can do or leave behind for small children. There are things that a parent can do. These things take planning and someone to help carry it out in the years ahead. It is nice for a child to receive a gift on a special day like

Christmas, graduation, a wedding day or a birthday. For very young children it is especially nice for them and helps them to feel a parent or grandparent's thoughtfulness even when they are gone.

Letters

Letters are perfect for occasions like birthdays or graduations or weddings. Maybe there would be special advice enclosed, appropriate to the occasion. Perhaps they could talk about themselves in the letter (maybe tell what their wedding/graduation day was like). The letters could talk about what your strongest characteristics are, what it was like on your prom night, or give some advice for a happy marriage. Talk about what you think makes a relationship work.

Jewelry

A nice tradition I've seen involves leaving/handing down to a child or grandchild a piece of jewelry – something you also received on the same date, like a 16th birthday for example. Knowing it once belonged to you, or that you bought it especially for them for this future event is a meaningful tradition.

Audio tape or CD

Record personal stories or maybe give advice that you wish your parents had given you at that age. I know of one man who left a whole series of tapes for his young son who was only 5-years-old when he died (he made enough tapes to give this boy one tape per year until his 21st birthday!). Each tape is different in theme and content.

Videotape

This is an idea that a friend might need to help with. Take a video camera to your favorite hang out spots. Share with your child the places that inspire you. Talk about what you have learned in life. Do a small tour of your hometown and places where you hung out as a child. Share the details of your past, your thoughts, and your dreams for their future.

*Being with those who are
slowly losing their life,
can be a quick way to find
a deep appreciation of what it
means to even have life.*

CHAPTER 21

SUICIDE AND EUTHANASIA

Our increasing technological capacity to prolong life forces us to discuss some complicated topics such as quality vs. quantity of life, traditional vs. alternative treatments and even suicide and euthanasia. Yet, as complex as some of these issues are, they are unavoidable in any full and honest discussion of the seriously ill.

The issues of suicide, assisted suicide and euthanasia are topics of increasing interest. They can turn a calm conversation into a passionate debate. Because of long held ethical and religious beliefs, it will undoubtedly generate intense discussion for many years to come.

Within our own country, the U.S. Supreme Court has recognized that there is no fundamental right to assistance with suicide, and it has turned the debate over to the individual states to resolve. While the legal status of physician-assisted suicide differs from state to state, only Oregon has made such assistance legal (in 1999), although opponents continually lobby to have the law repealed.

Outside the U.S., the Netherlands is one of the only countries to have lawful guidelines in place to help terminally ill people discuss, with their doctor, the ending of life once the dying process has begun. Critics of this feel it is a very dangerous practice, both ethically and practically. In 1990 there were 15 million people in the Netherlands, and 135,200 deaths. Of these deaths, 11,800 were euthanasia or "assisted" deaths.

Often, what motivates someone to want to end one's life is a desire to stop the suffering of mind or body. The feeling of becoming a burden to the family - financially or physically, feelings of embarrassment, loneliness, fear of uncontrolled pain, or the fear of living a life without independence, are all things that can play a part in the depressive decline leading to thoughts of suicide.

I once interviewed a 75-year-old man who had been diagnosed with prostate cancer and was near the end stages of this disease. He had spent his entire adult life working as a doctor (a pathologist). He knew he was dying and he didn't want it to drag on. So, he decided to take his life and he failed. I met him two months after he had failed and he discussed his feelings about this experience in detail. He said to me, *"I looked at my future and the future was going to be more pain, more limitation. I'm dying. My body is shutting down slowly. My eyesight is almost gone, my hearing is almost gone, one of the disks in my back is causing me a tremendous pain, and my wife died four years ago of breast cancer and she was my whole life. I accept the end of my life. I did try to kill myself but I won't do it again because the penalty for failing is too great. I realize now I was lucky, I could have made things much worse for myself. I've made up my mind, I'll never try to do it again."*

Without question, physical suffering is very difficult for most people to handle under the best of circumstances. If your loved one comes to a point where quality of life is gone, it can be a wrenching, tormenting experience both for the ill person and for their loved ones. However, even in the face of physical limitation, inability to communicate and great discomfort, someone who is seriously ill is still able to feel love, happiness and sadness.

All of the professional hospice workers I interviewed as part of the research for this book told me that it was common for people who are seriously ill to retain the ability to think, reason, communicate and feel emotions to the very end. The advantage of being aware of this, is that if you feel there is nothing you can do to help their outer, physical condition, there might still be something you can do to help their inner condition.

Whatever your feelings about the issue of suicide, it is clear to researchers and hospice workers alike: when a seriously ill person starts to feel like a burden to those around them it is easy for them to become depressed, and that will sometimes lead to thoughts of suicide.

BABY BOOMERS

The issue of "assisted suicide" will become more controversial as scientists create more drugs that enable us to live longer with disease. The present Baby Boomer generation (born between 1940 and 1964 – over 76 million in the U.S.) is the generation that will shoulder most of the burden of this research and the questions it will inevitably raise. Even now, many Baby Boomers are starting to care for their aging parents. Not long from now, they will be caring for their spouses or themselves.

As Baby Boomers begin to deal with the deaths of their parents, brothers, sisters, uncles, aunts, cousins, friends and spouses, increasing numbers of people will be forced to reflect on issues of death, dying, suicide and euthanasia. Here are some of the questions others have asked:

If my loved one should conclude that they want their doctor to end their suffering, by prescribing medications that would kill them, is it my place to protest that choice? When the end is obvious and inevitable, do I have the right to encourage a loved one to stay alive, even if it means constant pain for the next five to 10 weeks (or longer)?

What would it look like if the physician were given a role in helping patients to die, if they requested it?

What are the limits of human suffering? How much can a person take? When does courage end and inhumanity begin?

PALLIATIVE CARE

Palliative care, also sometimes referred to as comfort care, is primarily directed at providing relief to an ill person through symptom management and pain management. The goal is not to cure, but to provide maximum comfort and maintain the highest possible quality of life for as long as life remains. The focus is not on death, but on compassionate, specialized care for the living. For many people who are facing a terminal illness – and for their caretakers – turning to a hospice or a palliative care team is the option of choice, rather than seeking an answer through suicide, assisted suicide or euthanasia.

For more on palliative care and on topics associated with end-of-life issues, you may want to look online, or at your library for:

Innovations in End-of-Life Care (an international journal and online forum of leaders in end-of-life care) at:
http://www2.edc.org/lastacts/

National Hospice and Palliative Care Organization, or NHPCO, at: http://www.nhpco.org or call (703) 837-1500.

Physicians for Compassionate Care Educational Foundation, or PCCEF, at http://www.pccef.org/

Midwest Bioethics Center at http://www.midbio.org/ or (816) 221-1100.

Defining Wellness Through the End-of-Life at:
http://www.dyingwell.com/

Pain and Palliative Care Reporter at: http://www.painlaw.org/

Education for Physicians on End-of Life-Care at:
http://www.epec.net/

Growth House: Palliative Care (for hospice workers and care-givers) at:
http://www.growthhouse.org/palliat.html/

Palliative Care: Info Sheet for Seniors at: http://www.hc-sc.gc.ca/seniors-aines/pubs/palliative_care/pall_e.htm/

Seeking Answers and Dignity in the Debate Over the Right to Die at: http://focusonethics.com/excerptwhosright.html/

CHAPTER 22

LESSONS FROM
THE DYING

There are so many important life lessons to be learned from being with the seriously ill. Similarly, there are also many lessons that the seriously ill person learns from the journey. For some, illness is the friend that introduces them to their inner self, the inner world of spirit. So many of us spend our lives avoiding this look within, and illness can be a natural catalyst for looking inward. For others, illness is the teacher through which they learn the lessons of humor, patience, love and kindness.

They learn humor to ease their frustrations with their problems. They learn patience by having to deal with other people's misunderstanding of their journey and from being unable to do things they'd been able to do their whole lives without assistance; taking a simple shower becomes a complicated and, eventually, impossible chore to do alone. They also learn patience from having to deal with some aspects of our healthcare system which is sometimes less than perfect.

They learn lessons of love and kindness from people around them who care. These people reach out in simple, yet practical ways. Bringing food, renting movies or just *being there*.

While living in the monastery I became quite comfortable

around those who were ill and handicapped. One of the good works that monks, nuns and ministers do all over the world, is to try and help those who are sick and suffering. An important lesson I learned from this period of my life is that if you wish to work with the ill, you must learn to be at ease with someone else's difficult situation that you can't change. You must come to terms with your true powerlessness in life. While there is a lot you can do in life, there is so much you can do nothing about at all. For this reason, the serenity prayer becomes a mantra to many of those who are ill: *"Grant me the serenity to accept the things I cannot change, the courage to change the things I can, and the wisdom to know the difference."*

You can bring comfort and compassion into a situation, but you can't change the ultimate course of events even in the slightest way. You become a companion on someone else's difficult journey; a humble witness to the true state of what it fully means to be human.

It almost seems impossible to have a chapter called "Lessons from the Dying," without saying a word about lessons from nature. I believe it's important for caretakers to get out outside and into nature to relax and gain the perspective sometimes obscured in a hospital room, or at the bedside. Birth and death is the constant beat of nature's rhythm. And the more time we spend in the fresh air, in wooded areas, in the mountains or at the sea, the more we will gain a sense of peace – and feel the natural cycles of life, which includes death. Embracing nature as a partner, and making the appreciation of nature a regular part of our lifestyle, is one way to create a mindset that will aid us – and the people we care for – in the final days.

"Remember that when you leave this earth, you can take with you nothing that you have received – only what you have given."

– Francis of Assisi

ALTERNATIVE TREATMENTS AND FINAL THOUGHTS

I often contemplate the effects of modern technology on the future of medicine and serious illnesses, and wonder what medicine – and life – will look like 100 years from now. Even within 20 years scientists are hopeful we will experience tremendous progress in the treatment of disease, just from the breakthroughs we're seeing in DNA research. The way in which science and technology are paving the road of advancement is exciting, to be sure. Scientific research and experimental programs have largely taught us what we know about disease today.

There are many types of experimental programs for those who are seriously ill, but not many people actually sign up for these studies. Some statistics say that fewer than 3 percent of cancer patients sign up for any kind of trial study. This is partly due to the general public's lack of information about the existence of these programs. However, as the Internet increases in popularity, it becomes a more effective mechanism with which researchers can inform the general public of their work…if someone is looking.

By helping researchers, not only are many seriously ill people adding years to their lives, but they're helping their children and future generations by contributing to the body of knowledge we need to conquer various diseases. Joining an experimental program is not for everyone, however, and no one should feel pressure to join.

LIMITED ENERGY

Some people contract a disease and aggressively seek a cure by looking for the best, most promising doctor or experimental study. They may travel the country (and sometimes the world) searching for special doctors, physicists, shamans, healers, preachers, miracle workers, or medicine men in search of a cure. No one can criticize any one who tries with all their energy to find a cure. But, before someone aggressively seeks a cure, it is important that everyone be conscious of the toll that it can take on the rest of their energy – and their family life – when they return home.

The 30-year-old daughter of a man given four months to live, once told me, *"My dad spent his last few months flying all over the country meeting with specialists looking for a cure. He would come home and be so exhausted from the travel that he would stay in bed and sleep all the time. All I wanted was to go to McDonalds with him and eat a burger. But, I felt selfish at the thought of asking him to go out when he returned home looking so tired and sick. When it comes down to it, that's what I regret most. That was our thing. All I wanted to do was to go to McDonalds with my dad."*

Another person felt quite differently, when describing how he came to terms with his wife's cancer. *"When considering what course of action to take, Julie wanted to look hard at the facts and at the history of this specific cancer. We came to realize that in our case, the evidence pointed to the fact that time would probably be short and the side effects of treatment were very undesirable to her. At first, I wanted to try everything we could. But when I looked at it from her perspective, I understood why she chose to stay home and spend her time with family and friends. The odds were not good to begin with. Because of the thoughtful and open way in which she dealt with this, it became a powerful experience for all of our friends and family."*

Support your loved one no matter what they decide to do. For some people, fighting the disease does sometimes produce encouraging results and a longer, quality life. Just be sure the ill person is aware of the potential tradeoffs.

SPOUSES

One of the things a healthy spouse / partner can do to be of help to their sick spouse, is to place themselves in the sick person's shoes – and do it frequently.

A spouse of an ill person, can often be the one most intent on exhausting all possible options available for a cure. They are often the person on the Internet, researching until all hours of the night. They can be the one pushing for appointments with anyone who has had success in treating this specific disease; they can be the one arranging the travel schedule. Some believe this is how a good and loyal spouse should help. The problem is, they may never ask the sick spouse for direction on how they can help. It's often *assumed* that all energy possible should go into finding a cure. But how does the sick person feel about what direction should be taken? Is the sick spouse just going along with the other spouse, out of guilt? Since the healthy spouse is willing to put a tremendous amount of effort in helping to find a cure, why should the sick spouse attempt to tone down those efforts? Often, these unspoken assumptions and fears put more pressure on the situation. Neither spouse wants to let the other down.

It's important for the seriously ill person to be as free as possible when deciding what course of action to take. It's important that they are free to explore their ways of wanting to experience this journey of serious illness and possibly, this journey of the last chapter of life. Their way of wanting to go through this may include denial, drug therapy or visits to a voodoo priest. Whatever it is, give them the respect to do this their way, and ask them often to make it clear to you what their way is.

In the end, if the spouse does not ultimately beat the disease, this habit of asking *them* what they want, will take some of the pressure off of the caretaker. A woman once confided to me, *"When my husband passed away, I was haunted for years by thoughts of 'what if?' What if I would have suggested that he take the other medication? Would that have saved him? What if I would have given him more vitamins, maybe he never would have gotten sick in the first place."* It is common for these "what if" voices to haunt a caretaker – and there are no answers.

One possible way to circumvent these haunting voices is to never assume anything. Always ask the ill person how they would like a situation handled. How do *they* want to go about this? What treatments do *they* want? What doctors' appointments do *they* want? When care is taken to include the ill person in every decision that effects their life, the loudest voice you should hear, in the end, is not the voice of 'what if' but the voice of reason saying, *"We did our best and we did everything exactly the way he / she wanted it done."*

Remember, only when it is dark can you see the stars.
– Ani De Franco

CHAPTER 24

DISEASE, THE UNEXPECTED HEALER

Sometimes things happen in relationships that you don't fully understand or intend. All of a sudden, you wake up one day and you realize that you are as distant from a loved one as you can be. To make matters worse, you have no idea how to start back to where you once were in that relationship. So, you just sit there and do nothing – hoping that it will work itself out. But life doesn't usually work that way. Before long, we get busy and the weeks turn to months, the months to years, and the relationship has drifted like a raft on the open sea with no oar or sail.

Before my parents passed away, this had happened to me with one of my siblings. We were always very close, but for a period of a few years there was a distance in our communication. Then, mother's breast cancer came into the picture.

Somehow the difficulty of this situation built a bridge for us to walk on and meet each other. In that meeting nothing really mattered except that we had both walked toward each other on that bridge. Who said what, who did what, who felt what … didn't even matter. It was completely irrelevant and in the past.

The circumstance of an illness can be a great opportunity for healing, reuniting and reconciling some relationships. This might be one last chance to fix that relationship or at least make it somewhat better. If you have a family relationship that has floated along for years, this can be the opportunity of a lifetime. See it as a time when it's not too late. Sometimes, even in the worst situation imaginable, good things can happen.

FRIENDS

Another lesson often learned from this time in life is the importance of getting together with friends and loving family members. Friends feed each other's spirits. Only by expressing love, can we feel it.

As you have already experienced, there are many realizations that take place on this journey at the end of life. Often, people come to realize more fully how short life is (something many of us don't seem to fully understand until we lose someone close to us). This realization also helps us to focus on what is important.

You also may come to realize who your close friends really are. When I needed a ride to the airport to be with my mother, who was on her deathbed, I called someone I considered a close friend and explained the turn of events. I was surprised when she said, *"Oh, I wish I could drive you but, I'm just heading to my aerobics class. I haven't worked out all week."* Most of these "friends" dropped away.

Many people will say, *"Let me know if there is anything I can do."* Real friends are the ones who follow through, and often just show up without prompting. So, be prepared with a list of things that need to be done, when they offer to help. Remember, they may feel as helpless as you do, and their offer to help is something they *want* to do to feel less helpless and to honor the ill person; take them up on their offers. It's almost impossible to care for an ill person alone. *In the end, you get no points for martyrdom.* When someone asks and really wants to help, keep a list handy of things that will help you in your efforts: grocery shopping, errands, dry cleaning, feeding the cat, walking the dog, watering the plants, driving, bringing lunch, picking up the kids, cooking dinner, etc. Let people help if they want to.

If you find yourself caring for an ill person on your own, and you're feeling overwhelmed, call a local hospice for advice or support. Hospices all over this country have some of the most extraordinary volunteers that come in to help caretakers take a break from their caretaking responsibilities. Call them, even just to get out of the house for an hour or two.

Sometimes there are countless phone calls from people trying to find out the latest news. You might want to consider using your answering machine as a way to leave daily updates on your loved one's situation. This way, friends can find out the latest news in a way that will be less of a drain on you, and you won't have to repeat the same news over and over.

If friends want to drop by for a visit, or to help with something, don't hesitate to tell them when it's time for them to go. It's counter-productive to add more pressure to a situation that is already very stressful. If having a guest is not comfortable at any moment, ask for some space. So often, a seriously ill person will say, "Sure, stop by on Tuesday." Then, when Tuesday rolls around, they're not feeling up to any visitors. There is no need for the ill person to put themselves out in this regard. Just postpone or cancel the visit. It's not only OK to do that – it's the right thing to do.

Bottom line: don't be afraid to ask friends for help. Don't be afraid to set boundaries with them. They will understand. And if they don't, you will have learned a difficult but important lesson about which friends can be counted on in difficult times.

ANNIVERSARIES, BIRTHDAYS AND HOLIDAYS

The one month and one year anniversary dates of someone passing can be difficult for the people left behind. The same goes for birthdays, wedding anniversaries and holidays. Being with a friend on those days, who has experienced the loss, can be a great comfort. This person might feel particularly lonely or blue on that day and not even know why. A lunch, movie, or quiet time together are great ways to support the person experiencing the loss. Don't worry about what to say, or how to offer words of comfort. Just show up – your loving presence will be enough.

Walking the journey hand in hand with a seriously ill person is one of the most enlightening experiences any human can ever have. When you walk that journey with your heart open, you will never be the same.

QUESTIONS FOR REFLECTION

I think taking time to reflect on our lives is one of the most useful things we can do for ourselves. We all learn by our experiences and these experiences are what teach us and help us mature. When we take time to reflect and formulate our experience into words, we are then able to share our wisdom with others. Living with deliberate intention, growing awareness of one's true self, and reflecting on life experience are essential aspects of the maturing process.

In a book called *Questions... For Quiet Times* I have combined the concept of a journal with many thought provoking and soul searching questions. I wanted to create a tool that could help people reflect on their lives. If you have no idea how to begin to reflect on your own life, this book is a great way to start a meaningful conversation with yourself. Below are a few items for you to get started on. You may want to write these answers out in a journal:

• Write 3 or 4 pages about the experience that strengthened your character the most.

• What is the single most challenging aspect of your life right now?

• Write about five important or memorable people in your life and what you learned from each of them.

• What or who made you laugh hard over the past year?

• Describe your dreams for each of your children or grandchildren (if you don't have children, describe your dreams for a significant person in your life).

• God decides he will give you the honor of adding an eleventh commandment. What will it be? Explain why.

MEDITATION TAPE RECOMMENDATIONS

"Meditations from a Quite Place" by Dillon Woods

This 20-minute tape uses breathing, visual imaging and the sound of ocean waves to bring the listener to a place of peace and tranquility. Available at www.livingwithquality.com or by writing Windermere Publications, P.O. Box 25109, Los Angeles, CA 90025 310/358-6043

Leonne Schillo, R.N., M.N. is a therapist that works out of Beverly Hills and Malibu, California. She counsels those who have been diagnosed with cancer and uses her guided imagery tapes as an aid to reduce anxiety and stress (and thereby enhance the immune response). She has three tapes that she uses in conjunction with weekly appointments (which can be done by phone if you don't live in Southern California.). She can be reached at 310/457-3193.

Michaela Bohem is a hypno-therapist in Los Angeles. As part of her practice, she provides meditation, relaxation and support tapes for patients and families dealing with terminal illness. Her website is www.michaelaboehm.com and her number is 323/782-0878.

Dr. Carl Simonton is known the world over and has become legendary in his work with cancer patients. He offers many helpful tapes, seminars, retreats and books. Phone: 310/459-4994.

HIRING HELPERS

Many families may not need to hire help. But, should you need it, here are some tips on making the search easier and more successful.

Upbeat, Positive and Operating From The Heart

Look for people who are in a good place emotionally. Someone may do all the physical things the job requires, but they may not do it with as much heart as you know is needed. You'll be able to observe and feel - the difference quite readily.

Watch for Burnout

It's easy to lose that original inspiration that gets a person into a chosen profession, and nursing is no exception. There are so many difficult situations that make caring for the ill an incredibly stress-filled, difficult job. For someone to work with dying patients, with their heart connected to the situation, is, at the very least, draining and often times exhausting.

Intelligence

There should be a sparkle in their eye, a sign of life in there somewhere. If you are the loved one arranging the interviews, speak frankly about the situation and see if they have ever been in similar circumstances. Listen closely to what they have to say about their experience with past patients. See if the conversation between the two of you flows easily.

Chemistry

Introduce the nurse to the patient and see if there is any chemistry. When the nurse leaves, ask the patient how they felt about the person. There should be a strong level of comfort between a patient and nurse, as there are many intimate situations such as bathing and personal hygiene that are a regular part of their relationship. If possible, have the patient join you for the interview, perhaps giving them some specific questions to ask the nurse. Always try to include the ill person in the interviewing process.

Research - Letters Of Recommendation

Allowing a stranger into your home can put you in a vulnerable position, especially if you work a fulltime job. Ask for letters of recommendation and references, and be sure to call every reference, and speak to the people who wrote the letters to gauge how genuine their enthusiasm is for the nurse. People may say things on the phone (off the record) that they wouldn't necessarily put in writing. Don't forget to ask them to bring their nursing license with them to the interview. (Note: If you are using an agency to find nurses you might ask the agency what kind of questions they ask to screen nurses. Do they get a copy of their DMV record? Do they check references? Do they check for a criminal record? Do they check on licenses? Don't assume an agency has done any kind of background check, always ask questions).

Trial Period

Make it clear from the beginning that the first week is just a trial period to see how comfortable they are with the patient - and vise versa. Tell them you would like to try two or three different people. Don't just take any nurse. Screen them. Look for a person who meets your criteria and who connects with your loved one from the heart.

Driving Record

Should you need a driver, it would be reasonable to ask for a copy of their DMV driving record. DMV's won't disclose the information to you directly. But, you can request that they bring a photocopy of their driving record as well as a copy of their drivers' license. In most states, they can easily obtain a copy of their record by visiting a local DMV office and requesting it. This should be mandatory if they will be driving for you. Also get the name of their insurance company, policy number and call to double check the information. NEVER MAKE ASSUMPTIONS.

Variety of Agencies

The only people I have ever known to hire fulltime nurses were those who had unusually great insurance coverage or those who had money set aside to pay for it. It's very expensive! Some private duty nurses earn $300-$500 per 12-hour shift. If you are lucky enough to have 24-hour nursing care, it is usually split up between a team of nurses (teams may range anywhere from 3 - 10 people). If you have the money, it can sometimes be best to create a team with two or three nurses from a couple different nursing agencies (instead of six nurses from one agency, for example).

I once worked as a caretaker in a situation where one of the nurses was jealous of another nurse. In the end, the one nurse created a tremendous amount of political drama both at the patient's home and within the nursing agency. The agency was blinded by politics and in this case, the patient suffered. It could have been resolved more quickly if there were two agencies in the mix. Hiring an entirely new agency midstream is a lot of work and stress. You can avoid that by thinking ahead. If you have the money to hire several nurses, choose more than one agency and split up the days. If things go badly with one agency, you want to be able to leave that agency without upsetting the whole apple cart too much.

Good Questions to ask a Nurse

i. Who was your favorite, most memorable patient and why?

ii. Who was your worst patient and why?

iii. What do you like to do with your time while a patient naps?

iv. Rate your driving ability on a scale from 1-10 (with 10 being excellent).

---

v. What is the most unpleasant nursing task for you?

Another great idea is providing the nurse with a checklist. This will allow them to rate specific duties, with 1 being the lowest score - "I won't or have not been trained do this" and 10 being the highest "I can definitely do this." This way, you find out what they will or can do.

Can't Do - 1 - 2 - 3 - 4 - 5 - 6 - 7 - 8 - 9 - 10 - Can Do

- Light housekeeping
- Washing dishes
- Taking out trash
- Laundry
- Transporting from wheelchair to bed or car
- Outings
- Preparing meals
- Bathing / showering
- Cleaning vomit
- Range of motion / prevent skin ulcers (bed sores)
- Personal hygiene / skin care
- Changing diapers / peri-care
- Medications
- Tube feedings
- Dressing changes
- Suctioning
- Colostomy care
- I.V.'s

Caring for seriously ill patients can be a tough job. If you are taking care of a patient in your family home, there comes a time when you might want the support of professional nurses. I hasten to add, if a nurse is just going to come to you and stay for 10 minutes to see how things are going and supervise the situation, like hospice nurses do, that's a whole different circumstance. In this case, you wouldn't need to screen them in as detailed a manner, like you would if they were 24-hour nurses staying in your home.

But, if you want fulltime nurses, how do you choose one? In choosing someone to help, keep in mind that you need someone who can be a part of a caring team. The nurse needs to be a "can do" person - and comfortable being part of a team. So, look for secure, mature individuals who have positive energy and generous spirits.

Interview with as many nurses or aides as necessary (usually four to six is a good number to start with). It's always a good idea to take notes during all the interviews. When making the final decision, compare these notes. Saving them can also help, should you lose a nurse and at some point need to hire someone new.

HOSPICE WORKERS / HOSPICE VOLUNTEERS

This section provides helpful tips for those who may already be working in some capacity with the seriously ill.

Helpful Tips

Names

Upon meeting someone for the first time, it's important to repeat his or her name to make certain you have it correct and can say it correctly.

"Hi, I'm Mary."

"Nice to meet you Mary."

It is equally important to learn the names of family members and any significant people in the patient's life. Use someone's name frequently during the conversation. If you have a hard time remembering names, try using the word association technique. It really does work.

Sally has sand color hair; Denny has dark eyes; and Elizabeth looks extravagant.

Resentment

Be aware that from time to time the patient - for a variety of reasons - may resent your presence. Perhaps the fact that you need to be there at all, your mere presence symbolizes the seriousness of their situation, or they could resent your ability to have a normal life while they are in a steady decline. Whatever the reason, we all must be careful not to take things like this personally. It is all a symptom of how difficult these circumstances really are. The pressure can make ordinary situations very delicate.

Self Care

If you work regularly with someone who is seriously ill, it's important to keep some things in mind for your own comfort as well. Do not focus so much on others that you neglect your own self-care or the care of *your* children, family and friends. The best advice I ever received while being a caretaker was: take vitamins daily, exercise regularly, and take a long, hot shower (or bath) after a hard day. In other words, taking time for yourself allows you to give more to the person(s) you're caring for.

COMPENSATION

Compensation usually depends on what a caretaker's actual duties and experiences are. Are you just a driver? Just a shopper? Just a personal assistant? Just an accountant? Are you monitoring medications? Organizing doctor's appointments? Advising and guiding on personal issues? Are you in a position in which friends and family are also asking for your help, understanding and guidance? Are you doing all these things? Your salary should be commensurate with the level of skill and energy you put out.

In general, a fair place to start is agreeing that the salary increases as the responsibilities increase. This, of course, depends upon the stage at which you appear on the scene.

Whatever the situation, be sure you are happy with what you are getting back, because you'll be giving all you have - if you work with your heart open.

SELF-SEVERANCE PACKAGE

When it is all done, it's very helpful to have some money that you can fall back on for a while. When you work with your heart, you will need time to heal your own grief and resettle yourself. If a severance check is not an option in your situation, try saving just $25 a week for a "vacation fund" when it is all done. Use the money to spend a day at the spa, to take a long weekend away or even a whole week. This is a way for you to take care of and nurture yourself.

Burnout

Burnout says: you are giving out, more than you are getting back. So, when it feels like you are burned out, it's time to step back and do something for yourself. Sleep in. Take a day off and sleep as long as you want. Get a facial or manicure. Go to the beach. Go for a hike. Go out and blow off some steam on the dance floor. Go to a museum or a movie. Do whatever it is that you find fun, relaxing or interesting. Just be aware that the feeling of burnout is a warning signal that the situation has become unbalanced. When you spend all your energy caring for someone else, you must take time for self-nurturing and self-care.

What are some of the signs of burnout?

- Always tired.
- Don't want to be at work.
- You find yourself complaining and being negative frequently.
- You don't like the people you work with.
- You drive to work and say, "I don't want to go to work today."

Inventory and Reflection Time

What were the challenges for you during this time? Could you have handled a particular situation better than you actually did? What are the lessons for you at this time in your life?

Death forces us to be introspective. Use this time to think and use your journal to note all you are going through. It will help you feel better, when you are feeling disconnected. I know some people hate journals, but try it if you can on a regular basis, just a few minutes in the morning or at night. You'll be glad you did.

When we force ourselves to reflect by asking ourselves questions, we are coming in touch with unconscious thoughts and beliefs. It can be a very enlightening experience and very therapeutic.

Through someone's death, somehow, our lives are given a higher quality. To absolutely maximize this quality, we need to take time to reflect and let it sink in.

Questions for Your Consideration and Reflection

Please take a moment to read these questions. You may want to write out a short (or long) answer to each question. Or, make up your own questions.

If you keep track of your growth, in the years ahead you can read back on your life and feel encouragement as you see the progress of your own personal evolution.

i. What is the name of the person you have been working with?

ii. Name three of the biggest challenges in working with this seriously ill person.

iii. What are three positive lessons you have learned?

iv. What were some of the family dynamics you observed during this time?

v. How was your listening behavior? Did you listen more effectively than usual? Note both positive and negative examples.

vi. What can you do to improve your listening skills?

vii. Describe a time when your listening helped someone.

viii. Who did you meet during this time that was a really good listener? How would you describe them? What makes them such a good listener?

ix. Who did you meet during this time that was a poor listener? How would you describe them? What makes them such a poor listener?

LISTS AND CHARTS

There are various lists that you may need to keep track of the many issues that arise with caring for someone who is ill. Below are some suggestions to make things easier for you. The more small things you have organized, the less stress there will be overall.

- The first list to make is a grocery list. This is especially important if you are going to have non-household members do any shopping. I suggest typing up all your basic grocery needs and preferences – and then make multiple copies of this list. Then, when you run out of something, simply circle the item that you need. Such detailed organization will make shopping a breeze.

- When your loved one is in a hospital, it's important to have a family member close by most of (if not all of) the time. Hospitals can sometimes be curiously in-hospitable in its efforts to manage so many patients; it's easy for hospital staff to inadvertently make mistakes. Be on the lookout and be alert. Hopefully, those mistakes are not life threatening (like neglecting important medication). But, it helps to have a family member sitting by to watch and listen. Most patients appreciate someone else in the room with them as another ear. It's helpful for someone to make sure your loved one is getting everything they need. It could be considered a 'quality assurance' role. Patients often need an advocate for everything from double-checking the medications to asking questions when the doctor comes around.

Speaking of doctors, don't be afraid to ask lots of questions when they come around. This is another list to have close at hand. Usually, patients only have a few minutes with their doctor, so make every minute count. If your loved one agrees to it, get involved in the details of what doctors are saying. Understand what is going on. Take notes. If you met with an attorney, architect or your boss, you might bring a note pad. Do the same with a doctor. Treat the doctor's visit like a business meeting. If they know you are listening carefully and you are interested, they are likely to say more and explain things more carefully. Most doctors welcome that kind of effort and attention.

Finally, enough can't be said about the value of keeping a notebook in the hospital room, so family members can report to each other. This provides an excellent and easy tool for family communication. By describing things that have happened and making a list of questions as they come up, a kind of journal emerges. Having a family member that is very sick requires a team effort. This journal helps facilitate that goal.

People may be very thoughtful toward someone who is ill, with flowers and gifts. Do not depend on the ill person to respond by sending a thank-you note. They have other things on their mind. Put someone in charge of keeping a list of who is giving what, and if they have been thanked for their kindness. Flowers, cards, food dishes and gifts may be constant. People don't necessarily expect a thank you, or even a call to express gratitude for the kindness, but when it happens it's nice.

Person	Date Received	Message	Card?	Gift?	Flowers?	Respond?
Carl Jones	1-1-03	Get well	Yes	No	Yes	Yes 1/3/03

When someone is ill there can be many types of specialists, therapists, nurses, nursing agencies, pharmacies, doctors, and physical therapists involved. These next few items will help you keep on top of it all.

• Keeping track of who does what, and how to reach them can prove taxing. Stay organized and it will be less of a hassle when you really need them.

Doctor or professional	Kind of doctor	Office Asst.	Phone #	Fax #	Address
Dr. Smith	Surgeon	Kelly	555-1212	555-1212	123 Oak Ave. Suite 1

• There is usually a constant flow of drugs and as the disease progresses, the number of drugs may increase. This next chart will help keep it all organized. Keep all the doctors updated when there is a change. Doctors are infamous for not letting the right hand know what the left hand is doing. Keep on top of medications and don't hesitate to ask questions and point out contradictions (it's probably not your imagination). People make mistakes all the time.

Time drug is taken	Drug name	Milligram	Purpose	# tablets	Description of tablet
8 am	Dexamethasn	1 mg	Inflammation	1 tablet	Round-yellow

• Pharmacies: Keep track of what you have called in and with whom you spoke. Again, mistakes happen, but they might occur less often if you stay alert.

Pharmacy called on:	Spoke to:	Drugs/Supplies ordered

• There should be a main phone list of who to contact in case of an emergency or change in health. This would be a list of family and friends that the ill person would want to be advised of any developments. If possible, have the patient make this list with you.

Name of person:	Phone numbers (specify: work, pager, cell, and home)

• We all know that insurance companies can sometimes be confusing to deal with. It can be frustrating to track what they have reimbursed and what they have not. Even if you are pleased with your insurance carrier, you could still be served well by having one of these lists for each doctor or therapist that you see. You also may want to consider starting a checking account and/or a credit card account for healthcare expenses. This will make expenses easier to track, and instances of accidental double billing will be easier to rectify. If you've never been exposed to the accounting side of serious illness, you may be overwhelmed by how expensive it is to get sick. Diapers, lotions, medications, special food, doctors, pillboxes, cane, walker, wheelchair, and on and on. It adds up quickly. Keep track of it.

Check date	Check number	Check amount	Date of visit	Date sent to insurance	Amount reimbursed	Amount still owed to you

• If you have the ability and/or necessity to hire someone to help you with any of the details, it's important to keep track of interviews.

  i. Name

 ii. Phone number

iii. Referred by?

iv Finder's fee included for agency?

v. Weekly salary expected?

vi. Hours available?

vii. How flexible can hours be?

viii. Car issues:

a. Own your car?

b. Year of car?

c. Insured?

d. Cents per mile to be reimbursed?

ix. When are you able to start?

x. Green card issues?

xi. How close do you live to get here quickly in case of emergency?

xii. Comments:

xiii. After Interview Rating Scale (circle one)

Not so good - 1 - 2 - 3 - 4 - 5 - 6 - 7 - 8 - 9 - 10 - Very good

Please photocopy and fill in as needed.

Person	Date Received	Message	Card?	Gift?	Flowers?	Respond?
Carl Jones	1-1-03	Get well	Yes	No	Yes	Yes 1/3/03

Doctor or professional	Kind of doctor	Office Asst.	Phone #	Fax #	Address
Dr. Smith	Surgeon	Kelly	555-1212	555-1212	123 Oak Ave. Suite 1

Time drug is taken	Drug name	Milligram	Purpose	# tablets	Description of tablet
8 am	Dexamethasn	1 mg	Inflammation	1 tablet	Round-yellow

Pharmacy called on:	Spoke to:	Drugs/Supplies ordered

Name of person:	Phone numbers (specify: work, pager, cell, and home)

Check date	Check number	Check amount	Date of visit	Date sent to insurance	Amount reimbursed	Amount still owed to you

OTHER ITEMS AVAILABLE FROM WINDERMERE PUBLICATIONS:

BOOKS:

Where Souls Meet: Caring for the seriously ill $ 12.95 (paperback)
Questions... For Quiet Times $12.95 (paperback)

AUDIO BOOKS:

WHERE SOULS MEET: Caring for the seriously ill. $19.95
Cassette only, two tapes.

MUSIC:

Seasons - A CD of 13 original songs by Dillon Woods $14.95
"This ex-monk shed his robes, found God in a pair of jeans and turned poetry into easy listening. Seasons is uplifting, brimming with positive vibes... Woods has a nice voice and can spin poetry."
— *Dayna Cramer, BAM magazine (California's music magazine)*

RELAXATION TAPES: (for caretakers or those who are ill)

MEDITATIONS... From A Quiet Place (20 min.) $9.95
This relaxation tape uses breathing and visual imaging (with a back drop of ocean waves) to bring the listener to a place of inner peace and tranquility. Cassette only.

For Substantial Discounts on Bulk Orders for

Where Souls Meet: Caring for the seriously ill

Please Contact

Where Souls Meet
C/O Windermere Publications
P.O. Box 25109
Los Angeles, CA 90025

Phone: 310/358-6043
Please visit the website for bulk order pricing guide:
www.livingwithquality.com
